Presencing EPIS

A Scientific Journal of Applied Phenomenology & Psychoanalysis

2017
Volume 1

EPIS Press
2026 S. 9th W. #4
Missoula, Montana 59801 USA
epispublishing1@gmail.com
www.episworldwide.com
www.episjournal.com
www.episeducation.com
www.epispress.com

Presencing EPIS is published yearly as an online journal.

Printed in the United States of America
Library of Congress
1. Phenomenology 2. Psychoananlysis 3. Lacan 4. Existential psychoanalysis 5. Philosophy 6. Freud 7. Critical Theory 8. Gender 9. Adorno 10. Trans-humanist 11. Vivantonomy 12. Presencing EPIS

EPIS Journal is published as an on-line journal every Fall/Winter

Cover photo: Stock photo 272730429 | Globe resting in moss in a forest

ISBN 978-1-943332-11-3

Table of Contents

Letter from the Editor

Kevin Boileau, PhD

Each year that I write this letter for the EPIS journal, I am naturally inclined to review the state of the institute and its programs, including the journal. Institutes of this nature go through many growth phases, shifts and turns in mission, and a cycling of members as they make their own ways professionally. The Journal represents the noble attempts of various members and associates to put new ideas to pen hopefully to advance the field in some way. Our seminars and other educational programs are constant in their attempts to review old materials while forging into the new and unexplored. The radio show continues to open fresh discussion in a friendly, conversational style, some of which is published by EPIS Press. Yet, it is the EPIS journal that seriously participates in the triple-dialogues of phenomenology, critical theory, and psychoanalysis year after year.

The EPIS journal, Presencing EPIS, is peer-reviewed, of course, and represents exciting developments in the convergence of three powerful discourses concerning subjectivity. These discourses, each in their own way, push us to think against ourselves, a thinking that is vigilant and suspicious of what we believe to be true. This past school year, we started to focus on creativity and violence as we trudged forward in our investigations and searches. The topic of the 2017 journal issue reflects that. While this group of papers does not reflect all that could be said about these important topics and their related issues, they are important perspectives within these discourses, and the sort of participation EPIS expects.

Creativity is the cynosure of the new. It constructs, builds, and presences new thoughts, new attitudes, new behavior and, sometimes, new ways of being human. By definition, violence destroys what is, leaving both positive and negative effects, some intentional and some not. Yet, we can examine these effects historically, scientifically, and through the joint discourses of phenomenology, critical theory, and psychoanalysis, develop new understandings of the human anthropology and our future possibilities. It is a particularly fertile time for our inquiries, given that the world is in dynamic transformation, which has profound reverberations in self-structure, inter-subjectivity, and culture.

It is, therefore, with great pleasure that the EPIS Press and the EPIS journal release this 2017 issue of Presencing EPIS.

Kevin Boileau, PhD
Executive Editor
September 2017

Preface

Dr. Kevin Boileau, Executive Editor
August 2017

Preface: Trans-Humanist Considerations for Psychoanalysis, Critical Theory, and Phenomenology

I am writing this Preface to the 2017 EPIS journal with a sense of an immediate though placid approach. Because I don't need to be tendentious, or to write for personal interest, I hope that my comments will be appreciated for their intrinsic value to our communities. I believe that this is an important time for further transformation of psychoanalytic thought and clinical practice, for theoretical and applied phenomenology, and for students of critical theory. As such, I draft my comments with these potentials in mind.

This is also a productive time and growth period for any psychoanalytic training and research institute such as ours. The topic for this year's issue is creativity and violence, which is intrinsically important but also instrumentally valuable as an historical doorway for deeper investigation into the human anthropology and the sometimes-hidden models we assume in our theoretical and professional work.

I am chiefly concerned about the inner depth of human narcissism, egocentrism, and lack of positive regard humans demonstrate for our Earth and for all the non-human beings with whom we share space and biospheres. The sheer gravitas of the matter, therefore, propels us to look beyond mere human-to-human relationships and human clinical encounters for our material. As such, I would like to present what I take to be our basic autonomous, acquisitive human anthropology and challenge its efficacy and validity to operate as a model for psychoanalytic and phenomenological inquiry. I also point out that this is the model we have created historically. It is the model Freud was aware of and used, and the model that I believe has been at the bottom of the core of 20th century analytic and phenomenological theory and practice.

In its place, I shall offer preliminary ideas about a new model that can supplant the old. To this end, I shall focus on two main ideas, the first being vivantonomy, which rivals both autonomy and heteronomy as the basic relationship to the Other; the second a challenge to the common existential notion of being-in-the-world, which rejects a "one-world" thesis and replaces it with a "multiple world" assumption. In this investigation and argument, I shall integrate these two ideas with the intent of building a proto-statement for new paradigms in psychoanalysis that are no longer based on the autonomous self of the Enlightenment nor the outmoded belief that Dasein could ever be solely in that one world of humanism. This is the idea of a trans-humanist anthropology that leads to a trans-humanist psychoanalysis, phenomenology, and critical theory. It becomes a radically-reconstituted humanism with a different foundation.

In thinking about the progression from autonomy to heteronomy, toward an anthropology of trans-humanism, we are reminded of the early (Western) modern period, which valorized the development of the autonomous self, in which each of us lives in the world in terms of his own mental categories. In this tradition, we approach Others in terms of our own subjective interpretation of meaning and analyze Others relative to what we already know. It is an appetitive approach in which we consume Others by reducing them to the same cognitive categories of our own minds and experience. This prioritizes the subject over the object, and therefore creates an anthropological mistake. This leads to the problem of this essay: that we must shift the source of meaning from the subject to the object, but in a unique way. We will see in this text here that this idea is crucial for a trans-humanist position, requiring 1) a different noetic and 2) a different interpretation of the "objective." We already know how tempting it is for professional practitioners to rely on this paradigm, and how rewarded we can be by them.

By addressing this anthropological mistake, shifting the source of meaning to the object, and therefore developing a transcended humanism (a "trans-humanism"), we promote increasing levels of personal responsibility. By deepening levels of responsibility through the shifting of our Archimedean point, we reconstitute what we formerly thought of as "autonomy." It is now both humanist and trans-humanist, resting on a radicalized notion of heteronomy, concerning the Other. It is antithetical to many of the theoretical and value commitments of the 20th century and 21st century in psychoanalysis, and in other ways, to critical theory and to phenomenology.

To gain such perspective, we must, therefore, render a descriptive and critical account of the "I" of humanism, i.e., the masterful self that attempts to control and regulate meaning in terms of its own subjective categories. By looking at the received view of humanism in a new way, we can revise our humanism from masterful and controlling autonomy to a humanism of responsibility. This is the view that the "I" of humanism should be corrected by a deeper and more accurate anthropological-phenomenological account of the [intersubjective] self. Under this new view, the Other is foundational to the self. This creates phenomenological space for an interpretation of oneself that is not primarily motivated by its own appetite but instead is propelled by its absolute responsibility for the Other, toward every Other. This includes the trans-human. This is the non-human Other. This includes clients, patients, and non-humans.

By correcting the anthropological mistake of modernity, we can pursue a more accurate phenomenological understanding of humans, especially by focusing on our social dimension and interspecies dimensions. This can provide a foundation for a new ethics as well as provide a direction in value that could guide our social and political theory, science and philosophy. Derivatively, this leads to a new psychology, psychoanalysis, and psychotherapy; and new directions in both phenomenology and critical theory. This confronts us with question of how we construct, regard, and treat the ecology of the radical Other.

Let's think about solidarity by reconsidering the appeal of the Other. In this way of thinking, an individual's appeal stands in for all other people and all sentient beings, both ethically and metaphysically. This is the origin of solidarity in which we recognize that we are so deeply involved with one another that we are radically intertwined with Others; this leads to a radically deepened notion of responsibility, which I will address next. There is no inherent or good reason to confine the notion of the Face only to humans, or the appeal of the Other only to humans. Let me, therefore, explain what I mean. Phenomenologically, the eyes of other sentient beings, for example dogs or monkeys, have no relevant difference from those of humans. Look for yourself. Other animals have the same capacity to make an appeal, and they, too, have a Face. They, too, are universal examples of our wider community that goes beyond the human. We must, therefore, address the principles of solidarity and responsibility as they bear on a new approach to disciplines concerning human subjectivization and therapeutic practice. Otherwise, we risk our own existential fragmentation.

Solidarity comes from a recognition that the Other comes from the same community. In humanism, the community is the set of humans. In a trans-humanist approach the community is all sentient beings, and includes the whole environment—not just humans.

In this new perspective, the community is comprised of all sentient beings in the ecosystems of the world. A new understanding of solidarity articulates this. This idea is particularly important in analysis and critical theory, because we can all too easily create a self-Other, polarization even with the best of intentions, and even in the consulting room or the conceptual drawing board. A new examination of solidarity addresses this risk, which I believe can act as a corrective to ontological dis-parities, drawn by fiat.

In the scientific vernacular, by definition, all beings in an ecosystem are interrelated. In a spiritual-phenomenological vernacular, each sentient being has the capacity to make an appeal to this inter-related community of beings. To deny that all sentient beings ought to be included in a community of solidarity is simple deception, pathology, and existential distortion. It is like denying that I am alive. I have explained the reasons elsewhere, but they stem from narcissism. This is the not seeing what is directly in front of our eyes – a highly inter-related ecosystem. Nothing is separate. Human beings are not separate. Unfortunately, humans have been living as if they are separate. We have pretended that it is only our interests that are important and relevant; that we only have direct moral duties to other humans; and that we only owe duties to non-humans if they bear some relationship to the inter-human community. Yet, we should not be afraid to ignore the appeals of other sentient beings, and we should not be anxious about our dominating, possessory tendencies. This sickness has spilled over into the consulting room and the conceptual drawing board. Let's now address an understanding of responsibility that is informed by this new sense of solidarity.

Responsibility implies an awareness of all relevant considerations and then acting on them. In a humanist account, we focus only on humans and on other considerations, but only as they are related to our rights and duties, and the overall good of humans. Thus, we create and valorize a teleological, instrumental type of thinking toward any being that falls outside of the subset of humans. We create a hierarchy of being that projects an ontological disparity. This kind of thinking, however, creates permission to harm anyone or anything of perceived lesser value. Moreover, this type of thinking permeates inter-human relationships, too, unfortunately, some of them professional and social. In my judgment, this type of ontological perspective has profound effects on the total possibilities of our self-structures. This is the reason why it is relevant for any discourse that purports to study subjectivity and inter-subjectivity.

There is a deepening sense of responsibility as we move through the cultural valorizations of autonomy, heteronomy, and the radical revision that we see in theoretical constructions of trans-humanism. In autonomy, responsibility primarily comes from the law and is based on the reciprocal system of rights and duties that deter violent impulses. Heteronomy is a reversal of autonomy and deepens a rights and duties expectation by an underlying foundation of covenant. Here, my responsibility soars to all, within the human community without regard to rights and duties. Here, I act solely from my responsibility to my covenant, and to the priority of the Other. Yet, something is lacking and that is an anthropology and construction of responsibility that goes beyond the human; Its very foundation comes from a source more primordial and that is life itself.

This is an extraordinary—and radical—move that unsettles our humanism further as a new Archimedean point. Recall that we moved from geocentrism to heliocentrism in our epistemological understanding of the universe. We then came to understand that we are bounded by language and that within our cultural perspective, it is our semiological containers that propel and limit thought. Further, we see how Freud reverses Cartesianism by showing how the unconscious is master of our mental house, not consciousness. We also shift and increase human responsibility as we shift our understanding of the inter-human and inter-human dimensions. A trans-humanist argument, which proposes a vivantonomous starting point—a prioritization of life and not just the human—creates a foundation for responsibility that starts, not with the fact of being human but with the inherent and intrinsic value of all living matter, especially living beings who are sentient. Notice that I use "who" rather than "what." This is because each sentient being has a natural dignity based on its life, as gift from the universe, that is equal to the natural dignity of human beings, which is similarly based on their life as gift from the universe. There is no difference. This is ontological parity or ontological equality and it applies in both the inter-human community and in the intra-human community.

I propose two important points about this new understanding of responsibility. The first is that our understanding of the Other is deepened and broadened to include all life forms—all Others—especially those who are sentient, which are included in those beings whose face can appeal to us with vulnerability and need. The second is that as our understanding transcends both autonomy and heteronomy—their dialectic—that we come to understand that no being is Other, and everything is the Same. This comes from the truth that everything comes from the same origin, having a common root, and therefore, an ontological parity with everything else and everyone else. In this worldview, humans do not have a greater ontological value than other sentient beings. Thus, we extend our notion of responsibility, and we do this in a way that is both a quantitative change as well as a qualitative change. In short, we change ourselves. More formally, we reconstitute our subjectivity in the construction of a new human anthropology. What these new parameters are is somewhat vague and nebulous because this movement in our history is incipient and nascent. It is to this part of the equation that I now turn, hopefully to shed some light.

There are many species of beings that we humans will never see, and many that are in our daily ecosystems that we choose not to see. Yet, they are there—here—rather, constantly watching, looking, appealing—usually to we humans. We don't see them because of our own systems of value that are informed by our narcissism: our egocentrism. This type of consciousness therefore closes itself in on itself, not seeing other life, other humans, and our very selves. This is the possessory, dominating subjectivity that instrumentalizes all others, and even in a system indoctrinated by rights and duties, fails to see the Other's world on its own terms, as its unique manifestation. We understand all too well that an anthropology based on autonomy constantly struggles within the consciousness of a desiring, egocentric self. This is what leads to formulations and developments of heteronomy wherein I prioritize the Other over myself. Here are six basic axioms that I have laid out in previous work, but here also because of their importance.

First, we must dismiss the notion that humans are better, of more worth, or higher on a value scale. We must substitute it with a new axiom of ontological parity. This is for the reasons I mention earlier. This applies to all sentient beings. We are all equal. Second, we must agree that in principle that most of us have little knowledge about the whole: about how all beings, processes, and structures work together in an ecosystem. We substitute it with a new axiom of rigorous inquiry. This is a requirement for all of us, always. Third, we must accept a new Archimedean point. We cannot pretend to be at the center of the universe or the planet earth. This means that we must render an accounting of all life forms, including ours, holding that all living beings have equal interests and rights. We must, therefore, have an axiom that recognizes we play a part in the whole but are not the whole, and that we must mediate and weigh our interests relative to those of other life forms. This applies to inter-human relationships, too. Fourth, we must recognize that all life forms come from the same source. This leads us to the reconstituted notion of solidarity. This is a trans-human notion that includes the human equally with all other life forms, and that recognizes all humans are equal. Fifth, we must acknowledge and accept a new depth and breadth of our responsibility to others, including humans, other sentient life forms, additional life forms, and the environment in general. We must, therefore, try harder. Sixth, we must work diligently to formulate and articulate a new philosophical anthropology for human beings. This means we must strive for new meaning and understanding of the world and our place within it. This is neither the autonomous subject nor the heteronomous subject but it is a new human. This re-formulates the reality principle. It is the very reality principle we must interrogate and transform.

If we look at these six axioms together we can see that there is an isomorphism between individual narcissism (disregarding the Other human) and cultural/species narcissism (disregarding other life forms). Both include the same preoccupation with self or culture, and both ignore or actively trounce on the interests of Others. Moreover, we can see that there is an over-reliance on the law, which is a retreat to the familiarity of the superego position, i.e., the dominant proscriptions of one's society and culture. This is a denial of the transcendent in both the individual and in the social elements of a culture. There is also a compulsion to rely on the words used to taxonomically differentiate one type of being from another, which includes different levels of ontological value, rights, and protections. For example, in many jurisdictions wild animals are considered property, and become personal property once they are taken from the forest. This allows the human taker to do anything he wants to the "property." Analogously [and curiously], there are historical examples amongst humans, in cases of race and gender, in which different categories of humans were assigned different value. It is the same kind of thinking. Although this is a change in name, it is not necessarily a change in action although this might be the first step in a long-term, developmental process of change.

Where does this leave us with psychoanalysis? Phenomenology? Critical theory? Well, presently, even amongst senior members of these practices and theoretical traditions, there are individuals who cling tightly to the autonomous self of the Enlightenment. Thus, we often have egocentric selves ministering to egocentric selves coming for treatment. Theoretically, it is much the same, various claimants striving for dominance in dispersions of truth that are also regulated by egocentrism and narcissism.

I do not have the answers to these questions, but I think we should all carefully consider why psychoanalysis is effete without phenomenology, and why we need critical theory to correct insular notions of Dasein and human anthropology. We must interrogate even more deeply the question of the meaning of our human beingness; our understanding of the whole; how we live within our history but transcend it—how take a critical position toward what we think we know. This is ultimately a "thinking against oneself," which is one of the most difficult things one can do. This type of thinking always involves the Other, both human and non-human.

What I think can be most difficult, especially for senior theorists, psychologists, academics, and psychoanalysts, is how to bracket our commitments to our practices, our concepts, our training and experience, and our strong beliefs. I also believe that these strong beliefs and commitments place themselves within a constellation of autonomous, heteronomous, and vivantonomous worldviews—often sedimenting and fortifying our disability to enter new paradigms. In my experience, more senior professionals do it more than less senior professionals.

It is with these musings that I introduce this year's papers on the subject matters of violence and creativity, perhaps mutually originating from the same well spring. It is imperative that we learn more about the origin of our violence and our ability for creativity, to think our way to transcendence. As such, it is imperative that we consider a trans-humanist understanding and an approach that is based on the principles of vivantonomy.

Dr. Boileau

Author Bios

Johan Eriksson, PhD

Johan Eriksson is a psychoanalyst and psychotherapist in private practice in Stockholm, Sweden. He also has a Phd in philosophy and has published widely on phenomenology and psychoanalysis. Member of the International Psychoanalytic Association (IPA).

Michel Valentin, PhD

Michel Valentin is teaching French literature and textual/critical/ postmodern theory at the University of Montana (Missoula). Valentin teaches and applies Lacanian theory to the unravelling of any textual surface (graphic, written, filmic...). He also uses theory to enhance the socio-cultural critique of our contemporaneity and publishes in his area of expertise. He is a long-time EPIS member.

Robert S. Corrington, PhD

Robert S. Corrington is the Henry Anson Buttz Professor of Philosophical Theology in the Graduate Division of Religion at Drew University. He created the school of ecstatic naturalism. He is the author of twelve books and around eighty articles. His next book project has the working title of, "Spirit's Travail."

Loray Daws, PhD

Loray is a Registered Clinical Psychologist with the Health Professions Counsel of South Africa and a Registered Psychologist with the College of Psychologists of British Columbia, Canada. Loray serves as assistant editor for the Global Journal of Health Sciences, evaluator and international advisory board member of the International Journal of Psychotherapy (IJP), assistant editor and psychoanalytic candidate at EPIS (Existential Psychoanalytic Institute and Society). Loray supervises and teaches in South Africa, Canada, the United States, Australia and Turkey as faculty member of the International Masterson Institute.

Julio Roberto Costa, M. S.

Sociologist (M. S.), University of Brasilia, Brazil. As a graduate, studied Social Constructionism and relations between Cultural Studies and Psychoanalysis. Worked as a professor in many universities in Brazil. For 15 years, conducted field research on rural low-income communities, developing integrated actions with diversified social actors, such as farmer's associations, local governments, unions, NGOs and social movements. Conducted in-depth studies of the work of Otto Rank, whose books he became acquainted with still as an undergraduate student.

Gary Kolb, PhD

I am a therapist and have worked full-time at Harbor Crest Behavioral Health hospital inpatient treatment center for chemical dependency for 15 years. I have both a PhD and a Psy.D. and have a private psychotherapy practice. I am also a psychoanalytic candidate at the Existential Psychoanalytic Institute and Society. I have been married for 43 years to the same woman, raised 8 adopted children, and re-assemble old car parts in my spare time.

Daniel Green, PhD Candidate

Daniel Green is a PhD student in Philosophy at University of California, Riverside. His research interests include 19th and 20th Century Continental Philosophy, Philosophy of Religion, and Critical Theory. He maintains a daily meditation and yoga practice.

Freudian Psychoanalysis: Truth, Self-knowledge and Psychological Development

Johan Eriksson, PhD

Abstract

The psychoanalytic clinical endeavour acquires its form and character toward the background conviction that truth is the food of the soul. But how are we to characterize the form of knowledge and truth that is sought for in the psychoanalytical process? And why would knowledge and truth pertaining to our own spiritual life automatically entail our growth and development as human beings? The author tries to answer these questions with help from, first of all, Heidegger´s phenomenological investigations of the concept of truth. The imperative of truth in the psychoanalytical context, the author argues, is a fundamental demand that the interaction in the consulting room should as far as possible be of such a character that it promotes the possibility for the patient´s psychological expressions to *speak the truth*, to *fulfil its own claims.* The truth we strive for in the psychoanalytic process is thus not primarily centred around knowledge in the classical, epistemological sense but is rather about a *way of being and living.* Truth, in this context, is an *ethical* concept. And since the genuine form of psychoanalytic self-knowledge is created only by a subjectivation-process that transfers the unconscious impulses and possibilities into the sphere of truth, the psyche must, in this process, start to *respond*, to become *responsible*, and to thereby enter into a movement of *re-organization*.

Keywords: Sigmund Freud, Martin Heidegger, truth, self-knowledge, psychic suffering, defence mechanism, the unconscious, first person authority

Introduction

In a frequently cited text, the British psychoanalyst Wilfred R. Bion states that "healthy mental growth seems to depend on truth as the living organism depends on food." Whenever truth is lacking or deficient, Bion continues, "the personality deteriorates" (1965, p. 38). I imagine this to be an intuitive truth to most people. And for us psychoanalysts it is more than that: our whole clinical endeavour acquires its form and character toward the background conviction that truth is the food of the soul.

In several of the foundational texts of psychoanalysis, Freud repeats this emphasis on truth, making it clear that we should see truth as a technical imperative to all psychoanalytical treatment. Here we may think of such statements as "the analytic relationship is based on a love of truth – that is, on a recognition of reality – and that it precludes any kind of sham or deceit" (1937, p. 248), or "psycho-analytic treatment is founded on truthfulness. In this fact lies a great part of its educative effect and its ethical value. It is dangerous to depart from this foundation" (1915, p. 164).

In the secondary literature, it has been common to refer the *pathos* for truth that permeates Freud's clinical texts to his epistemological positivism, to his conviction that psychoanalysis is a science and embrace "the scientific *Weltanschauung*" (Freud 1932, p. 158). Here, it often sounds as though Freud would have transferred a passion for scientific truth into the area of clinical treatment of the individual. I don't think this view stands to scrutiny. On the contrary, I imagine that Freud's own passion for scientific truth found nourishment in his conviction that psychological health and development presupposes that we leave behind the infantile omnipotence, and the direct and hallucinatory satisfaction of infantile wishes, to the benefit of the sublimation of the drives and the adjustment to a hard reality. For Freud, therefore, the scientific age represents the highest stage in the psychological and cultural development of mankind. The scientific man, so Freud thinks, is ideally characterized by his doubting all ideological authorities, by not being seduced into regarding himself in animistic or religious terms; in short: by letting his emotions, projects and his gaze upon the world and himself be governed by the actual state of things, not by his own or other people's wishful thinking.

The passion for truth is thus not, in Freud's case, a kind of love for science itself. It is even possible to stretch this thought to imagine that the quest for truth is not, in the first place, to be characterized as a fundamental facet of psychoanalytic treatment which strives to promote the development of a better life – as if the quest for truth were subjected, for example, to a kind of *emancipatory interest of knowledge* (Habermas, 1968). Rather, the quest for truth ought perhaps to be seen as a *central, constitutive aspect* of what psychoanalysis defines as a good life. In this way, psychoanalytical theory and praxis could be seen as an expanded articulation and development of the very general intuition which reveals itself most clearly in the fact that it is almost conceptually impossible to imagine a dynamic and flourishing life based on lies and deceitfulness.

The experience of truth—in philosophy, this is called "evidence". The situation of present day psychoanalysis has become somewhat ironical in this respect. Psychoanalysis has been marginalized due to an accusation for not being based on evidence, despite it being the singular form of treatment that makes out of the experience of evidence its central, therapeutic moment. Freudian psychoanalysis is the only form of psychotherapeutic treatment whose essential idea and ethos are built up by truth and evidence, and we can thus safely hold psychoanalysis to be the only genuinely evidence-based form of treatment on today's therapeutic market.

The ambition of the present article is, if not to give a full answer of the involved questions, so at least to open a path that could lead to an answer of how, on the basis of the founding works of psychoanalysis, we are to analyse the content of Freud's intuition that truth is the food of the soul. In what way is truth connected to psychological development? Or, to be more specific: why would insights into our own psychological life automatically entail the growth and development of this life?

But before I try to answer these questions, I must ponder a while over the fundamental and not easily answered question: what is truth?

Truth and Correspondence

Even the briefest examination of our everyday use of the concept of "truth", and its related modifications, reveals it to be far from univocal. Sometimes we speak of a true friend, or a truthful person. Sometimes we speak of true art, true love, true fear, etc. We speak of true or genuine gold and we speak, of course, of theories, thoughts, convictions and statements as being true.

Despite these wide ranging applications of the concept of truth, however, the main tendency in philosophy has always been to start with theories and statements. When we enter into theoretical reflections, so it seems, theories and statements immediately present themselves as the natural and fundamental cases where "true" and "false" become relevant judgements. And this is closely related to another natural tendency, going all the way back to Aristotle, which is to think of truth in terms of correspondence, i.e. a statement, a thought or a theory is true if it corresponds to an actual state of affairs.

The so-called correspondence theory of truth—formulated in many more or less convincing versions—has of course been contested over the centuries. One of the most influential attempts at problematizing it was Martin Heidegger's. In the famous § 44 of *Sein und Zeit* from 1927, Heidegger claims that although there is a kind of justification for the correspondence theory of truth, we must liberate ourselves from our crude ways of understanding the concept of correspondence. We must ask ourselves: in the correspondence between a thought or a statement and a state of affairs, what is it that corresponds, really?

This question, Heidegger continues, cannot be settled by arbitrary speculation. Rather, we must take as our starting point, in accordance with the phenomenological attitude that characterizes Heidegger's investigation, a real experience in which the truth of a statement *reveals itself.* But where are we to find such an experience? The short answer: we find it when the statement gets confirmed as true. This is thus called "evidence". Heidegger gives a very basic example (1927, p. 217f). Assume that somebody with his back turned against the wall made the correct statement that the painting on the wall does not hang straight. The truth of this statement is confirmed when the person turns around and observes that the painting actually doesn't hang straight. But *as what* is the truth of the statement revealed in this confirmation? Is it really revealed as a correspondence between the statement and the state of affairs?

In order to reach an answer to this question, Heidegger in the next step asks what the utterer of the statement is related to when he, without seeing the painting, makes his statement. It would be a kind of falsification of the phenomenological content if anyone claimed that the utterer is related to an image or a representation of the real painting on the wall. According to Heidegger, the uttering of the statement is not related to anything else than the painting itself. The uttering of the statement *lets the painting be seen* as tilting to one side. The uttering, in Heidegger's words, "discovers" that toward which it is directed.

And now we can understand that in the confirmation of the truth of a statement, in the experience of evidence, truth is not revealed as a correspondence between two separate phenomena—the statement and the state of affairs, the thought and the thing—but rather reveals itself as a correspondence between the state of affairs *as discovered through the uttering of the statement* and the state of affairs *as confirmed through the act of observation.* The truth of the statement, what is confirmed, is that the statement reveals the painting *as it is in itself.*

If we use the terminology of Heidegger's teacher Edmund Husserl, who of course deeply inspired Heidegger himself, we could say that, in this case, the perceptive confirmation of the truth of the statement, its evidence, means that we have been able to give the statement a "intuitive fulfilment" (*Anschauung Erfüllung*). But now, the statement is a phenomenon of such a character that it can be true without us having any justification of its truth. We can conclude, then, that the true statement is characterized by the fact that it *can*, in principle, gain intuitive fulfilment. The true statement fulfils, so to speak, *its claims* (in this case the claim that the painting tilts to one side). The false sentence, on the contrary, lets the being get seen, but *not as it is.* It *ascribes* something to the being that the being itself lacks, and is thus principally unable to gain intuitive fulfilment. In contrast to the true statement, it does not fulfil its claims. It speaks in an *empty* fashion.

To Fulfil One's Claims

If we leave Heidegger's analysis of the truth of statements to one side, we can still conclude that the formal structure he conceives seems to be generally applicable, rather than being restricted to phenomenon such as statements, thoughts and concepts. That something qualifies as true or genuine gold, for example, at closer inspection means precisely that it "fulfils its claims". How are we to understand this?

The wedding ring on my finger is not primarily a dead, material thing characterized by its extension in space and its ability to resist pressure. In its capacity of being an artefact within a human and normative context where such things as love and sexuality are organized through the forming of families and through marriage (with its formidable arsenal of established rituals and symbols)—in other words, in its capacity of being inserted into a "world"—the ring has *meaning* and *significance.* The ring *speaks,* in a wide sense; it "tells us something". And what it says is, among many other things, "I am made of gold". The ring *makes a claim,* and *therefore* it can be made of genuine or false gold: it can fulfil its claims, or not. Any piece of metal cannot be genuine or false gold. A piece of metal must first speak, as it were, the language of gold. A piece of metal which did not speak the language of gold—for example a random piece of metal I found in the forest—can on closer inspection reveal itself as gold, but by the time I found it, it wasn´t genuine or false gold: it just was—gold. Only when the piece of metal starts to show itself *as gold*—only when it has starts to make "gold claims"—will the logical space be open for questions such as "is this really genuine gold?".

The same formal structure will of course apply when we, let´s say, call somebody "a true friend". To enter into that sphere where somebody can have the character of being a friend that can be true or false, the behaviour and attitude of my friend must first of all speak the language of friendship. Once this language is established, a certain action on his part, e.g. that he takes a day off work just to help me moving, may show him to be "a true friend". In this case, my friend shows himself *as he is.* His actions "fulfil" the claims that his general attitude towards me has established. Had he not helped me but instead made up a bad excuse for not doing it, I might have considered him *a false friend,* i.e. someone who makes the claim in his general attitude of being a friend, but who then fails to fulfil it through his actions. He then, in his general attitude, *shows* himself, but *not as he is.* An arbitrary person in my social network may indeed lie to avoid helping me moving, without ever running the risk of being "a false friend".

But now let´s move closer to our actual problem: when we go to emotional states such as love, fear or anger—what is it that makes it possible to call them true? Again, it is that they fulfil their claims of being true, that they show themselves *as they are.* In accordance with its inner character my fear of snakes, e.g., claims to be true or justified by the fact that it develops within a network of beliefs and expectations where it gains its character of being precisely a fear of snakes. The fear must harmonize with the belief that snakes in one way or another is dangerous, that they maybe are present in the environment where I am, that they may attack under certain conditions, etc. Were it not for this network of beliefs and expectations (which justifies the fear) the fear would cease be precisely fear, and we would stand before something else, e.g. an outburst of phobic anguish (and we are speaking of logic now rather than emotions). The fear´s claim of being fear—its language of fear—would be false, empty.

The same, again, with my love for philosophy: it is in the nature of love to claim to be true, or as we say—authentic. Had my fascination for philosophy not been guided by a warm joy and a genuine appreciation of philosophical challenges (i.e. things that indicate my love's claim to be exactly love), had it instead been founded by vanity or a wish to live up to my parents' expectations, then my engagement would show itself as something it is not. It would not fulfil its claims to be love. To expressions of love would then be false.

Questions of truth and falsity may engage people to a smaller or greater extent. It has something to do, of course, with what subjects they concern, what your vocation in life is, what your beliefs are, what your particular areas of invested interest might be, etc. For the goldsmith, it is crucial to know that his material is genuine, while another person may have inherited gold and pearls that he would never bother to examine any closer. A scientist is of course deeply engaged in the truth-value of his theories and hypotheses, while another person gladly reads a popular science magazine without being awake at night racking his brain over whether the discoveries he read about are true or false. However: when it comes to engagement in questions about our own spiritual life it seems not to be conditioned in the same way. Here, I agree with the philosopher Raimond Gaita (2002, p. 237-241) when he says that we are unable even to imagine a person who is totally indifferent to the truth and falsity of the deeper facets of his own soul—if his love, grief or ambition is real or fake, if they are just hollow echoes or if they fulfil their own claims and expressions. That such questions continue to trouble us seems to be *constitutive* for the very concept of a human being, a personality, a soul. Most of us would surely agree that if somebody displays a complete indifference to what is real and fake in his interior life, then that person has indeed "lost his soul".

This stated, it has become time to approach our guiding question: why does psychoanalysis hold truth to be the food of the soul? Why would we, having gained psychoanalytic insights into the truths about ourselves, automatically grow and develop by virtue of such knowledge?

The Imperative of Truth

The classical, Freudian psychoanalysis is thus subjected to an imperative of truth. But what kind of truth are we speaking of here? Is the main object of the imperative to demand of the psychoanalyst that he abandons all sentimentality and emotionally supportive interventions to the benefit of making correct interpretations of the analytical material, thereby really helping the patient to reach new knowledge about his own psyche? Maybe. Personally, I think the following way of putting it is more appropriate: the imperative of truth in the psychoanalytical context is a fundamental demand that the interaction in the consulting room should as far as possible be of such a character that it promotes the possibility for the patient´s psychological expressions to *speak the truth*, to *fulfil its own claims.*

The truth we strive for here is thus not primarily centred around knowledge in the classical, epistemological sense—as if the success of the therapy could be measured in terms of the amount of knowledge about his own psyche the patient has managed to acquired—but is rather about a *way of being and living.* Truth, in this *ethical sense*, is in itself the reason for the analyst to abandon sentimental sympathy and conciliatory kindness. And this is also the condition for judging *all interventions from the analyst's side* in terms of their truth—not only interpretations in the classical sense. An intervention—an interpretation, a humming, a spontaneous association, a question, a confirmation of what the patient has just said, a tactfully placed silence, etc.—is true if and only if it promotes the development of truth as a way of being and living. This means, perhaps surprisingly, that an interpretation might be deemed false even if it happens to be correct in terms of the involved psychological and historical facts. Indeed, if an interpretation is put forth at the wrong time, or if it is given in a form that is insensitive to the patient's level of cognitive and emotional development, it does not promote the development of true expressions, but might instead run the risk of being used by the patient for defensive purposes—let´s say for purpose of developing a kind of intellectualized and superficial "self-knowledge" which in the end becomes part of what Donald W. Winnicott has termed "a false self" (1965).

Naturally, I do not wish to discard the thought that self-knowledge is the basic therapeutic aim of psychoanalysis. On the contrary. But as soon as we start analysing the imperative of truth, we also find it necessary to ask the question of the nature of the involved self-knowledge in a more nuanced way. To get further in this task, however, it has become necessary to first say something about the psychological suffering which psychoanalysis, in Freud's original sense, is supposedly able to cure exactly by virtue of the genuine increase in self-knowledge that it ideally involves.

Psychic Suffering

It would lead too far to go through all of Freud's etiological analyses of ways for psychoneurotic suffering to arise. On a formal plane, it will be enough for us to conclude that Freud generally conceives of psychic suffering as closely related to the concepts of "defence" and "resistance", and the list is well-known of what he calls "defence mechanisms": repression, projection, introjection, reaction-formation, regression, isolation, negation, splitting of the ego, etc.

In Freud's theories, psychic development does not come forth as a regular and law-bound process that automatically continues along the same tracks as long as the inner and outer conditions remain relatively intact. Rather, he holds the psychic development to be determined by how well the psyche manages to handle the inner and outer challenges that the human psyche must invariably encounter (the most famous of them being of course the Oedipal Conflict). Psychic development, it might be said, is in itself a psychological achievement. This means that the psyche must be thought of as an organization that essentially remains *vulnerable.* Aided by more or less primitive defence mechanisms, the psyche has tried to handle the inner and outer challenges it has faced. Some parts of the psyche may have developed prematurely, while others may have lagged behind on more primitive levels. By way of repressions and reaction-formations certain impulses may have been referred to the unconscious, while a punishing super-ego was formed to control these impulses. Painful experiences of being small and needy may have been projected on to an outer object, while an ideal of self-sufficiency may have been internalized to constitute the kernel of the inner organization of the ego. To put it briefly: to perceive psychic development in terms of psychological achievement means to imagine the psyche and its expressions as something multifaceted and multilayered, something that is split into parts that are on different levels of development, forming their own agendas and seeking, idiosyncratically, to form their own kind of expressions. It is the lifelong assignment of the psyche to orchestrate all these disparate parts into a unity where there in the best case prevails at least some kind of cognitive, moral and emotional equilibrium.

All this makes it understandable why Freud reaches the firm conclusion that even if a person's suffering is closely related to certain actual circumstances, for example that of a painful divorce, the suffering would still not take on the specific form of psychological *symptoms*, or of being a *psychoneurotic* suffering, if it were not for the fact that the actual experience has an emotional relation to, and thereby awakens, infantile conflicts that were earlier dealt with in a deficient way. The defence mechanisms that the psyche activates under the actual circumstances, and that helps us explain the symptoms of suffering, does thus always have their prototypes in the infantile life.

Furthermore, we must reach beyond the thought that the defence mechanisms are focused solely on keeping ourselves not conscious of e.g. a forbidden aggressive impulse or an incestuous wish. Rather, the defence mechanisms should be seen as different attempts at refusing to *identify ourselves* with its content.

Take for example the defence mechanism that Freud calls "negation". According to Freud, this mechanism entails "a way of taking cognizance of what is repressed; indeed, it is already a lifting of the repression, though not, of course, an acceptance of what is repressed" (Freud, 1925, p. 235f). Or think of a projection where you are acutely aware of what you reject, but you remain completely unaware of it *belonging to you.*

The "de-subjectivation" accomplished by the defence mechanisms explains why the unconscious parts of the psyche have a tendency to remain on lower levels of development and why they fail to get integrated in the relatively reality-adapted structure of logically interrelated wishes, beliefs, desires, convictions, expectations, etc. that form the more mature parts of our personality. The unconscious aspects remain dissociated from the organization that would bestow them with meaning and direction. Unconscious thoughts, wishes and emotions, thus, differ from their conscious equivalents not only by the lacking the specific quality of "being conscious" (in that case they would belong, in Freud's terminology, to the category of "pre-conscious" rather than the category of "un-conscious"). The difference is more dramatic, since the unconscious stratum is composed of inchoate and primitive forms of what we normally call thoughts, wishes and emotions. Primarily they have, you could say, the character of "impulses" or unrealized potentials.

The ability of the defence mechanism to de-subjectify, viz. to stop thoughts, wishes and emotions *from forming*, also explains why the unconscious aspects of the psyche are so entangled in what Freud calls the primary process, which represents the most primitive and original way of psychic functioning. As the unconscious impulses and potentials remain unintegrated and dissociated they stand in a loose and *associative* rather than logical connection to content of the more reality-adapted parts of our psychic life. These impulses, therefore, are not expressing themselves in a rational way, but rather in a *symptomatically* and to a large extent disguised way. As the emotional cathexis of the impulses are displaced to elements in the actual world (I here refer to both the inner and the outer world),—a world that is thereby invested with unconscious and multifaceted layers of meaning—psychic and physical actions in and in relation to this world may take on a quality of satisfaction that the mature parts of the psyche have a hard time to identify and experience. To borrow a famous example from Freud (1917): the depressed person's loud complaints about his own worthlessness is revealed to express, at closer inspection, an aggression toward a lost object that the person has been unable to mourn, internalizing it instead as a part of the ego. Or think of the example of an intelligent and sensitive man that seeks the analytical help with diffuse relational problems.

His clear and seemingly productive self-reflections during the analysis might later be revealed as a kind of disguised and obsessive urge to anticipate the analyst's interventions, and to thereby make the analyst feel superfluous. The man's seeming eagerness to cooperate might in time reveal, in a number of ways, an unconscious and hidden tendency to confirm an auto-erotic and anal-sadistically tinged feeling of superiority or self-sufficiency—a tendency that has turned his love life into a troublesome story.

The suffering psyche, in psychoneurotic sense, is thus fundamentally characterized by *confusion,* by always speaking ambiguously, by being, in Freud's words, "out walking in a country one does not know" (1937, p. 237). The suffering psyche is unable to collect itself and to set a firm direction concerning the basic, emotional orientation of its life. In short, the suffering psyche, in psychoneurotic sense, does not speak *the truth,* does not fulfil its own claims. The suffering psyche *show* itself, but not *as it is.*

On the basis of these characteristics we may conclude not only that our psychic suffering manifests something untrue, rather it does something more than just that, viz. it manifests a discarded truth, an act of *avoiding the truth.* Due to our ignorance, we are often able to state, in earnest and with no intention of lying, false things about actual state of affairs. This, however, does not seem to apply to our distortion of the deeper aspects of our own psychic lives, even though this kind of distortion is mostly not conscious. The defence mechanisms are not so much *causes* of our psychic suffering—as e.g. me having slept bad might *cause* my inability to listen attentively to what you are saying—rather, they represent the *form* of suffering, as e.g. jealousy can be the form of my present inability to listen to what you are saying (cf. Gaita 2003, p. 99). At closer inspection, the psychic suffering will always be revealed as *ethical suffering,* and thus the psychoanalytic treatment, with its attempt at recovering the truth, should finally be seen as an ethical cure where you are not, primarily, facing traditional epistemological tasks, but rather are facing assignments such as *opening up, admitting, confessing, becoming sincere, becoming truthful* (cf. Eriksson 2014).

All this being said, we have started to line out some answers to the question about how we are to understand the kind of self-knowledge that we are striving for in psychoanalysis, and we have also begun to understand how knowledge and truth concerning our own psychic life entails the development and growth of this psychic life.

First Person Authority and the Unconscious

A central, constitutive aspect of what it is to be a person, a subject or an "agent" is the fact that you have a first person-perspective when it comes to your own psychic life. In the philosophy of psychology one to talk about this in terms of the subject having "first person authority" in relation to its own inner states: if you want to find out what I want, what I believe, what I am thinking etc. I am simply the best person to ask. I can speak about my mental states with an authority that is lacking in other people´s description of me. Someone else may find out what I want and believe by observing my behaviour and listen to what I am saying, but I can know these things about myself, as it were, *directly*, without having to base this knowledge on external observations. You may ask me why I am angry, but it would be very strange for you to ask me how I can know that I am angry.

This, however, does not necessarily mean that our subjective knowledge about our own psychic life are automatically transparent or without flaws. There are of course many occasions in life when others may understand me better than I do myself (this is quite a common experience and not something that psychoanalysis invented), but if this was a *general* fact, if it happened *always*, I would lack the very core of what constitutes me as a person or a subject – a subject that can sometimes in error about himself, or maybe have built up a self-image that is to a large extent false.

But what does the first person authority actually *consists of*? One way, traditional but increasingly criticized, of answering this question is the following: I can speak of the states of my own psyche in virtue of having a privileged epistemological access to them. My mental states are in a specific region of reality that I am the only one to have direct access to. By means of my inner perception, my introspective gaze, I can directly perceive something to which others can only infer on the basis of external observations.

Two of the most ambitious and thorough attempts at questioning this so called "Cartesian" view of the first person authority have been presented by Richard Moran (2001) and David H. Finkelstein (2003). These authors hold, correctly, that the Cartesian view does not do justice to the fact that first person authority is based rather on the fact that my mental states are precisely *mine*, something that *I am*, that they are deeply embedded in my character, my history and my ways of understanding and relating to the world. This entails that I am not only able to speak *about* my mental states, but I am also able to express them, and to express them as I speak about them. When I say "Charles is jealous", I do not express Charles' jealousy, but when I say "I am jealous", this is more than a mere statement, it is an *expression* of my jealousy. Thus, first person authority in relation to my jealousy does not mean that in virtue of having an inner perception I can be in a privileged way *conscious of* my jealousy, but rather that I can be *consciously jealous.*

On the basis of this discussion, we may now widen our former characterization of the Unconscious as Freud understands it. The unconscious aspects of our psychic life—that we formerly defined, not as not conscious, but as de-subjectivized and undeveloped—are primarily characterized by the fact that we cannot *express* them, in a direct fashion, by admitting them and ascribing them to ourselves (cf. Finkelstein, p. 119). When it comes to my unconscious jealousy, for example, it is fully possible that I can be aware of it (my analyst has maybe convinced me of feeling it), but that I am still unable to *jealously* say "I am jealous", and, in that way, express my jealousy and let it fulfil my statement.

However, even as *I* remain unable to express the unconscious, it will still find *its* expression. The unconscious always finds its expression (were it not so, there would be no justification for talking about something unconscious), but when it comes to the *form* of its expression, it diverges sharply from the conscious aspects of our psychic life. One of Freud's most important terms for the particular forms of manifestation of the unconscious is "acting out", a term that is intimately related to what Freud has called "compulsory repetition" (1914). As we have seen earlier: the unconscious impulses cathect in a disguised manner our psychic and material environment (e.g. the therapy-room and the analytical relation), transforming it to an infantile tinged scene where the impulses may be *acted out* in the form of psychic symptoms and as symptomatic behaviour.

Psychoanalytic Self-knowledge

A psychoneurotic suffering soul is thus, to a large extent, "acting out" rather than "expressing itself". It is confused in the sense that it cannot back up its own manifestations; it is so to speak ruled by "its psyche", viz. it is ruled by something that the subject "has", something that has not been integrated and developed enough to take the form of being something that the subject in a full sense of the word "is".

All this makes us able to say that Freudian psychoanalytical treatment—which formal aim is to "make the unconscious conscious"—is all about extending and encouraging the patient's first person authority, extending the patient´s possibility of speaking *from himself*, expressing himself, of speaking and living *truthfully*. Thus, the genuine form of self-knowledge to which the psychoanalytical treatment aims must have the character of a "subjectification process". This Freud realized at an early stage. The analyst's attempt at increasing the patient's knowledge of himself will remain useless until the patient has come to take it on as an *assignment*, a delineation of a subjectification process he must go through *himself*. Or, as stated in Freud's more spatially oriented metaphor: the patient must use the analyst´s message "to help himself in discovering the unconscious complex *where it is anchored* in his unconscious" (1909, p. 121). A few years later Freud speaks about "[t]he strange behaviour of patients, in being able to combine a conscious knowing with not knowing" (1913, p.142). And in his introductory lectures, we read such statements as: "there are different sorts of knowledge, which are far from equivalent psychologically"; and: "there is more than one kind of ignorance" (1915-17, p. 281).

What Freud is after here, I think, is the experience that, to be able to assume its transformatory ability, self-knowledge must really become genuine *self*-knowledge rather than mere knowledge *about oneself.* And it must be achieved through a process where *I* participate by *opening up, acknowledging, admitting,* etc. Self-knowledge, as Freud understands the term, "must rest on an internal change in the patient such as can only be brought about by a piece of psychological work" (ibid. p. 281).

But finally, why would this kind of knowledge concerning our psychic life automatically mean that this psychic life grows and develops? Why do we grow by confronting ourselves and our own unconscious? We have already lined out an answer: self-knowledge means that we expand our first person authority and our ability to express ourselves *from ourselves*, to express ourselves *truthfully.*

Regression and Re-organization

The ideal psychoanalytical treatment is often defined, in a somewhat programmatic fashion, as a two-part process of "regression" and "re-organization". I consider this general characterization to be quite true. The therapeutic framework of psychoanalytical treatment—the frequent therapy sessions, the asymmetrical relation between analyst and patient, the armchair/couch-setting, etc.—are all there to help the patient regress, to provoke his unconscious impulses to seek associative derivations and satisfactions in the therapy room, i.e. in the transference-relation to the analyst. Here, the specific competence of a talented analyst will be defined in terms of a sensitivity for the distorted and secretive expressions of the patient's unconscious in the transference, and in the same time an increased sensitivity for the ways in which the patient's conscious claims have become hollow or false. Secondly, the competence of the analyst will consist in his ability to convey his impressions to the patient, carefully and with the right timing, thereby facilitating a process where the unconscious impulses gradually start showing themselves *as they are.* All in all, we are here speaking of a kind of regression, a form of re-vitalization of the infantile layers of the patient's psychic life.

We may say, somewhat schematically, that what we encounter in this process of regression is a kind of total turning point or shattering. According to Freud's theory, the unconscious layers of our psychic lives become de-subjectivized and un-developed not because they are *too painful*, but because they threaten the unity of the psychic organization that forms the conscious part of our personality. When I, through the psychoanalytic process, start to get contact with my unconscious, when the unconscious gradually reveals itself as *belonging to me*, an uncanny form of disorganisation will take hold. When e.g. my need of love and care comes to the fore, the *emptiness* of my conscious claims to be self-sufficient is revealed, together with the emptiness of all the thoughts and fantasies that are supposed to support and justify these claims. The organization of my personality, in the defensive and rigid form that I have developed, has begun to fall apart.

At this point of the treatment, at this point in the regression—it is of course not an isolated instance but a segment of a process that is often of the "one step forward, two steps backward" kind—it becomes possible for the psyche to reactivate what Freud calls "the irresistible advance towards a unification of mental life" (1921, p. 105), i.e. the *re-organisation*. As the unconscious impulses and possibilities begin to assume the form of thoughts, emotions and wishes, that are then admitted to be *my own*, as they thus start showing themselves as *being something*, as they start to *make claims* rather than just acting in secret, they also enter into the sphere of truth. We may recall what we said of gold earlier: the question "is this genuine gold?" enters into the logical sphere of truth and falsity only when a certain piece of metal has begun to *behave and show itself as gold.* At an earlier stage, on the level of undeveloped impulses, the unconscious has been acting solely in regard to pleasure and un-pleasure, satisfaction and the lack of satisfaction. Now however, as the unconscious enters into a relation with the other strata of our psychic life—now when I can start to say e.g. "I am jealous" in a jealous way, now when I start to express myself—my whole psychic life will be forced to respond to questions that is placed outside the sphere of mere pleasure, but inside the sphere of the good life. Here, we encounter questions about such things as justifications, values, beliefs, doubts and obligations: is it right for me to feel like this? Is it justified? Can I stand for this? Who am I? Is this what I want. Why am I thinking like this? Is this really me?

These formulations convey a perhaps overly intellectual version of a process that is often not so much that, but as a way of indicating the content of the emotional facets of the psychic re-organization I imagine them to be sufficient. In the ideal case of re-organization, Freud thinks, some impulses and aims will be abandoned as anachronisms, and their cathexis will be retrieved, integrated and re-directed towards more reality-oriented goals. Other impulses might develop further and force me to modify my understanding of my own identity, to leave behind the rigid beliefs and fantasies I had built up as defences at an earlier stage. Put briefly: since the genuine form of psychoanalytic self-knowledge is created only by a subjectivation-process that transfers the unconscious impulses and possibilities into the sphere of truth, the psyche in its entirety must start to *respond*, to become *responsible*, and to thereby enter into the process of development where my spiritual forces are gathered in an emotional organization through which the expressions of the *psyche* can take the form of being the expressions of the *person*, and thereby can start to *fulfil their claims.* Without truth, as Bion has rightly claimed, "the personality deteriorates ". And this is finally not an empirical but rather a conceptual truth, an insight into the essence of being a person.

References

Bion, W.R. (1965) *Transformations.* London: Karnac Books.

Eriksson, J. (2014) "Freud´s psychoanalysis: a moral cure." *The International Journal of*

Psychoanalysis, nr 4, vol 95: 663-675.

Finkelstein, D.H. (2003) *Expression and the Inner.* London: Harvard University Press.

Freud, S. (1909) *Analysis of a Phobia in a Five-Year-Old Boy.* S.E., 10

- (1913) "On the Beginning of the Treatment. (Further Recommendations on the Technique of Psycho-Analysis I)". S.E., 12.

- (1914) "Remembering, Repeating, and Working-Through. (Further Recommendations on the Technique of Psycho-Analysis II)". S.E., 12.

- (1915) "Observations of Transference-Love. (Further Recommendations on the Technique of Psycho-Analysis III)". S.E., 12.

- (1915-1917) *Introductory Lectures on Psycho-Analysis.* S.E., 15.

- (1917) "Mourning and Melancholia". S.E., 14.

- (1921) *Group Psychology and the Analysis of the Ego.* S.E., 28.

- (1925) "Negation." S.E., 14.

- (1932) *New Introductory Lectures on Psycho-Analysis.* S.E., 22.

- (1937) "Analysis terminable and Interminable". S.E., 23.

Gaita, R. (2002) *A Common Humanity.* London, New York: Routledge.

- (2003) *Philosopher´s Dog*. New York: Routledge.

Habermas, J. (1968) *Erkenntnis und Interesse*.Frankfurt a. Main: SuhrkampVerlag.

Heidegger, M. (1927) *Sein und Zeit*. Tübingen: max Niemeyer Verlag 1993.

Moran, R. (2001) *Authority and Estrangement*. Princeton: Princeton University Press.

Winnicott,D.W. (1965) "Ego distortion in terms of the true and false self". *The Maturational Process and the Facilitating Enviroment: Studies in the Theory of Emotional Development*. New York: International University Press: 140-152.

Gender Urinary Segregation and Political Correctness[1]

Qui quae vult dicit, quae non vult audiet.[2]

Michel Valentin, PhD

Photography by Meghan Nolt—Montana Kaimin.

Alternative signs hang over the plaques marking both the men's and women's restrooms on the third floor of the UC during the "Gender Expansion Conference" on Saturday, March 20 2015. The sign reads "*all gender restroom—without urinals—anyone can use this restroom regardless of gender identity or expression.*"[3]

Introduction: The Premise

The comprehensive list of LGBTQ+ Vocabulary Definitions *Guide to Gender: The Social Justice Handbook*, elaborated under the guise of safety (Safe Zone project), anti-victimhood, and respect for difference, was put together by Sam Kellermann.

Motivated by a desire to help "people make sense of the alphabet soup," and be as respectful and accurate as possible when using "sexual identifying language," Killermann presents himself as an activist, educator, and artist. He is also "Director of Creativity for Hues" (a global justice collective inspired by the Rainbow coalition—he uses the same "colors metaphor") who created sites such as, *The Safe Zone Project* (a free online resource for LGBTQ awareness and "ally-ship" training workshops). He is the author of a TedxTalk, "*Understanding the Complexities of Gender*," and wrote *The Sexualitree* (a comprehensive sexuality model and curriculum, with downloads), *Singular They*, as well as the *Sexual Orientation for the Genderqueer Person*.

For Kellermann's "show and tell" "LBGTQ+ project," desire is similar to the alphabet soup (the author's metaphor) whose spoon-full our mothers used to try to coax or cajole into our mouths when we were toddlers.

Each swallow of the liquid letters which peppered the breast's milk substitute was accompanied by an a-l-literal, pouting bubbling and smeared stumble which, Mommy, with a careful spoon swipe would re-introduce in our mouths.

Semes of mushy, written language, bits and pieces of Mommy's voice, attention, and gaze, i.e. a literal morsel-ling of her body, are all mixed randomly in this apparently simple semiotic soup of pre-Oedipal desire until we, pushing the envelope to test Mommy's love, shove the bowl over the high-chair's edge.

The oral drive, the desire to please Mom, the apprenticeship of language and reading, and the *fort/da* game of our anxiety about Mommy' love and availability, highlighted these 'precious' moments when Daddy was not yet around, not fully in the picture (and in full regalia), when the "*name-of-the-father*," the grand "party pooper" did not exert his rule to split the monomial relation into a binomial one.

Of Monom, Binom and Polynoms

Likewise, the alphabet soup allegory used by the *LBGTq+ project*, explicitly and implicitly asks us to return to the privileged time when individualized letters were free-floating around in what Freud would call a "primary" (short of primeval) soup, randomly caught by the motherly spoon, forming beforehand a pre-text similar to what Freud called the "polymorphous perverse," Kristeva, the "*genotext*," and Deleuze and Guattari (positively) " chaosmosis."

This brew is monomial and could later produce a polynomial serialization of sexual expressions/orientations, à la Sam Kellermann, if, and only if, the incest taboo did not interfere, i.e. if there were no unconscious, no Other. This monomanial origin could be the retroactive originator of powers of variables (as full-fledged identities) if, and only if, the negative integer exponent (*the name-of-the-father*) did not exist or was excluded; if the phallus (signifier of the lack) was not the only signifier capable of designating "*as a whole the effect of there being a signified*" (which is a semblance of course, but a necessary semblance).[4]

In other words, for sexual-identity performers the monomial child-m(o)ther is a retroactive, fantasy-product, itself producing Imaginary variables with repetitions (hence the Facebook and LBGTQ+' s 40+ sexual identities—all variations on the same and variables of the monomial "One+"). The problem with such a pluralist and "serialist" production of sexual identities is that an "Other" does interfere with the "One +" (i.e. the m(o)ther-child) in order to produce the future dyad m(o)ther and child *and* binary sexual identities and not a polynomial series. The Real (Lacanian meaning) of sex realizes in the present its own past, which bears testimony to lack, castration and unconscious

Otherness—not consciously chosen others. In Lacanian theory, the LBGTQ+'s alphabet soup would correspond to what Lacan calls the *object a.*, i.e. what lies at the core of the fantasmatic identity of the subject.

So the LBGTQ+'s "liquid letters" metaphor is well chosen since it unwittingly (?) underscores/underwrites a basically anti-Oedipal project—for good or bad reasons/motivations; meaning, is it a progressive step forward in the march of human liberation by freeing desire from contingency and arbitrary oppression, a searching process inventing new narratives of desires with no precedent in our cultures, or a regressive path making everybody its/their/theirs/his/ze/zir/her/zee/zerr/ zeer... own Imaginary's prisoner, the result of a naïve, short-sighted logic and confused sentimentality?

The LBGTQ+ project sexualizes a-posteriori the original, monomial letters of Mommy's soup by attributing to each infantile iteration and re-iteration an identity during a period when the toddler's lack has not yet taken any signification: hence the 40 + repetitions/declensions or variations on the same theme, and the confusion between expression and identity (or "structure" and "style" to use Lacanian psychoanalysis).

Since the LBGTQ+'s alphabet letters are supposed to decline the whole gamut of the alphabet of desire, away from any paternal metaphor or "signifier of the lack," this is why not only do the project's authors have to invent a "third sex,' but also a myriad others as well (see the list in the endnotes). The list pretends to be neither comprehensive nor "inviolable." It is a work in progress because, according to the LBGTQ+ understanding of sexual reality, sexual identities are growing every day and even could be numbered by the thousands. Why not? The sky is the limit. "To each according his desire" is the motto of capitalism which makes us regress to this "ideal," Imaginary state when each consumer is baby-like, following the whimsies of the day, and where any object (things, animals, plants, forms, machines, monuments...) can becomes the support and consume the fantasy of the consumer, i.e. letters which can be bought and exchanged—no longer the Letter of a "*père-version*," but an inscription of the momentary, transitory (governed by the "here-and-there" and "now-and-then") version of the "*vers*" (towards), which is the trans/trance-movement of desire itself..., towards its implosion:

"*Very gradually, sexual life comes to an end the way it began. Having awakened first to dreams before coming to reality, it is in the end returning to the fantasy, to the imagining of the first sexual objects—like the fetishism connected with the first arousals in one's immediate milieu.*"[5]

From Alphabet Soup to Crusty Pie or Having One's Cake and Eating it too

The American anthropologist and queer theorist Gale Rubin goes the extra mile by presupposing sexual life as a circle with "*a charmed inner circle*," constituted by binaries such as couple/alone, or in groups, monogamous/promiscuous, same generation/cross-generational, bodies only/with manufactured objects..., etc., and an outside, forbidden, out-of-the-inner-circle area, were the sexual life escaping binary gender restrictions and compulsory heterosexuality exists.

With Mimi Marinucci, this circle becomes a pie, of infinite dimensions, or at least able to be infinitely divided (remember Zenos' paradox):

"*Rubin's circle can be thought of as an infinitely divisible pie. Divided into enough slices, it is hard to imagine that there is anyone whose sexuality would not be situated on the crusty outer edge of at least some of those slices. Crusty is deviant. Edgy is queer.*

In this sense, everyone is a sexual deviant in at least some way or another.

In this sense, everyone is at least a little queer, even those who are further from the edgy crust and closer to the gooey center on that one slice of the sex pie that represents the contrast between heterosexual and homosexual pairing."[6]

The idea is to liberate "sexual expression" as an object of desire from any constraints of figuration and return it to the pure Imaginary play of forms, a primary multi-directional onanism which wants to pass as a sexual communication ("expression"). To achieve this goal, "sex" must be detached from any prescribed bodies, from the idea of a hidden governing (unconscious) structure, from a more rigorous and radical objectivity (the one provided by psychoanalysis for instance). It must then be tailored according to the whimsies of the customer-host, in order to accommodate any appearances and resemblances, any affinities, likes or dislikes, which are then essentialized via a name and a practice, and then (final step), turned into identities.

The *Guide* is therefore constantly being honed and adjusted for language, since sex-identities pop up here and there, like mushrooms on a rainy day. According to its author, the definitions must "resonate" with at least 51 out of 100 people who use the words. The Guide is democratic, since it is governed by a "majority vote of one." Since sexual identity terms are tricky, the *Guide*'s author cautions us to be careful because a description that works perfectly for everyone using that label simply isn't possible (one cannot help wondering why! And also, if Killermann is serious or just having fun while laughing all the way to the bank!). Since it is an ever-evolving project, like a dictionary, the *Guide* is updated every four months.

Rationale and Discussion

There are many reasons why "sexual identities" proliferate today and are perceived by many as being as flexible, modular and changeable at will, as if made of rubber; as if the pleasure principle was a moveable, plastic feast.

The first one is the tendency of the financial and socio-economic fluxes of neo-capital to de-territorialize 'everything' (produces/products, objects, materials, and the physicality of the world, as well as human emotions and affects), to use a Deleuzian concept.

The second is the tendency, directly related to global capital, to de-essentialize, "de-nature" and "format" socio-cultural-economic life's materiality, so that its different aspects can take on the logic of a commodity, can be marked and imprinted with the linguistic sign's logic (coded by the System), and thus be easily inscribed/inserted in the grand carrousel of commodities by circular permutation while obeying the law of exchange-value dictated by the standard arbitrator/referent of equivalence, the monetary sign ($, Euro, Yen, etc.).

Both tendencies transform the binary sign/object opposition/difference mediated by the reference function into something new. The sign then becomes a pure signifier detached from any signified and traditional modes of reference or referential (the Lacanian Symbolic system). This gives to the socio-cultural environment of consumerism a flexible, moveable dimension. The effects of the variability/flexibility/mutability of signs not only directly inform the fluidity and volatility of desire but plug themselves into it. In Lacanian term, one would say that the drive of capital (the circular exchange, fluxes and flows of financial capital and commodities, counter-clockwise or clockwise accordingly, like the paths of hurricanes between the West and the East, the North and the South, America and Asia...) puts desire into over-drive, plugging directly the Imaginary into the Real with minimum (or strongly reduced) interactions/mediations from the Symbolic.

The gender proliferation espoused and promoted by the LBGTQ+'s logic obeys more the logic of erratic excess and the cultivation of pleasure generated by late capitalism than the logic of liberation, progress and emancipation. Neo-capitalism has already more or less eroded any totalizing normality and replace it with its own based on drift, erring, estrangement, de-construction, de-territorialization, change and speed. The gender proliferation inscribes itself into the same flux. It is not a genuine, progressive cultural revolution but an acting out responding to the cultural multiplicity of revolving intensities generated by consumerist capitalism, as Slavoj Zizek explains in his book, *Organs Without Bodies*, while taking on the Deleuzian philosophy which pretends to use neo-capitalism as a forward, liberating march into the future. Deleuze and Guattari, with their *Anti-Oedipus*, aimed at making the Oedipus complex (cornerstone of Freudian psychoanalysis) which they deemed reductionist, obsolete by complexifying it, making it implode by saturation, and then use the processual enrichment yielded by the ensuing implosion to feed the newly released energy into virtual lines of bifurcation, of differentiation, of rhizomic expansion via lines of flight and molecular lines opposed to the molar lines of institutionalized concepts. Their ultimate goal was the destruction of homogeneity, universalism and totality in the name of a "fractal ontology" of heterogeneity which would liberate and provoke the emergence of individual potentialities.

The problem is that it is exactly what postmodern capitalism has accomplished and is still accomplishing since the 1980s. Zizek makes it clear via a detour using Jean-Jacques Lecercle's parabole of the yuppie reading Deleuze and Guattari's *What is Philosophy* on the Paris metro, in his *Pedagogy of Philosophy*:

> *"What, however, if there is... but enthusiasm, when the yuppie reads about impersonal imitation of affects, about the communication of affective intensities beneath the level of meaning ("Yes, this is how I design my publicities!"), or when he reads about exploding the limits of self-contained subjectivity and directly coupling man to a machine ("This reminds me of my son's favorite toy, the action-man that can turn into a car!"), or about the need to reinvent oneself permanently, opening oneself up to a multitude of desires that push us to the limit ("Is this not the aim of the virtual sex video game I am working on now? It is no longer a question of reproducing sexual bodily contact but of exploding the confines of established reality and imagining new, unheard-of intensive modes of sexual pleasures!"). There are, effectively, features that justify calling Deleuze the ideologist of late capitalism. Is the much celebrated Spinozan imitatio afecti, the impersonal circulation of affects bypassing persons, not the very logic of publicity, of video-clips, and so forth in which what matters is not the message about the product but the intensity of the transmitted affects and perceptions? Furthermore, recall again the hard-core pornographic scenes in which the very unity of the bodily self-experience is magically dissolved, so that the spectator perceives the bodies as a kind of vaguely coordinated agglomerate of partial objects. Is this logic in which we are no longer dealing with persons interacting but just with the multiplicities of intensities, of places of*

> *enjoyment, plus bodies as a collective/impersonal desiring machine not eminently Deleuzian?"*[7]

The vogue of sexual categories started with pleasure and consumerism and is directly linked to the affirmation of gay counter-culture and queer theory. It first started in gay clubs to facilitate the *drague* (cruising/ picking-up/hooking-up) so that one's sexual preference (conflated here to "one's specific way of coming") could be communicated quickly to minimalize time-loss (searching for the "right partner"), and maximize "quality-time" (enjoying the "right" partner). For instance, if a gay male likes to be penetrated but also likes to have the upper hand in a relationship, he would say or wear a badge with the inscription *"cismale gay power-bottom."* The preferences, categories, and positions linked to *jouissance* were created to attract the adequate partner who would/could then plug into the *dragueur's*/searcher's specific desire.

These literally emoticons-like, little consumerist signifiers, then tended to take on a life of their own. They became independent propagated and propelled by the energy of the market. With consumerism, seduction itself was not spared. It became the capital seduction to be marketed as well as the capital(ist) seduction of the market itself. Inverting the passage from that which functions as a general structure to that which functions as a singular tendency, the partial logic of these partial signifiers turned the hierarchy upside down, trying to enthrone categories while dethroning the unifying principle. The problem is that human sexuality does not escape the incest taboo and wo/man binary **sexuation**; as Lacan said during the 1968 French Cultural Revolution *"structures do not walk into the streets."* That is to say, one cannot take one's desires for the reality.

Pluralism of Choices Against Binarism

One of the first effects of this quasi-law-like mutability in the sexual domain is to increase the arbitrariness of what is already arbitrary (as Lacan explained) with regards to the sexual divide.

In his XXth Seminar (*Encore*, 1972–1973), Lacan, (nicknamed the "French Freud," although Lacanian praxis—theory and clinical practice is more neo-Freudian), theorized sexual difference as a "**sexuation**" (complete with a graph prefaced by a few of his famous "mathemes" derived from formal logic and theory of sets) depicting the non-biological (or beyond biology to be more exact), "de-"naturalized, subject-positions of masculinity and femininity. Lacan purported to uncover an inherent, unconscious-governed, subliminal and ineliminable structural difference or discrepancy and gap separating the binary sexes. This quasi-law depicts an inescapable tragic, structural logic, condemning speaking human beings and sexed subjects not only to be inherently split within themselves (as to the, origins, causes and effects of their desires), but also to being essentially, necessarily out-of-sync with each other (something women have complained about for millennia). Lacan summarized this structural impossibility with his now famous sentential declaration: "*Il n'y a pas de rapport sexuel*" (There is no sexual relationship between the sexes).

This makes the "gender divide" appears more uncertain, and therefore constraining and unnecessary, something consumerism was quick to focus on. Gender, then, had to be submitted to the law of exchange-value and to what appears/ seems to be the rule of individual choice and self-determining subjectivity.

This subversive "negative capability" of postmodern capital seems to illustrate, satisfy, and fit, at first glance, the Deleuzian liberating rule of de-territorialization, and the Lacanian maxim of the ethics of psychoanalysis: "*the only thing of which one can be guilty is of having given ground relative to one's desire.*" (Lacan. *The Ethics of Psychoanalysis.* 314.) In fact, is not one of the Master injunctions of capital, conveyed via advertising, to obey or follow one's desire, enjoy now and pay later? And since we do know that the power of a body is measure in terms of affects, the liberation of affects from the destiny of the body and the liberation of bodies from the rule of affectual gendering should liberate bodies and affects for capital—using the pretext of personal freedom as an incentive (the whispering mode of the snake in the apple tree—so that everybody can have their cake and eat it too.

The price to pay, of course, is the short-circuiting of the Symbolic system to the advantage of the Imaginary which is freer to reign supreme. The whole question is the following: is this a true liberation? What is the ultimate price to pay? Does this bring us closer to an ultimate liberation from rules and constraints, allowing the emergence of a more authentic self, of a Nietzschean type of post-civilization wo/man, or of a Sadeian type of individual?

Is the de-substantialization of gender the result of the postmodern rule of neo-capital? Its cultural by-product? Was gender rule the genuine origin of the general sexual malaise and oppression felt by many of our contemporaries? Is our contemporary "liquidification" of sex and gender the liquidation of gender-oppression? Does this liquefaction really escape gender-rule? Is living one's sexual desire (bi or homosexual) a real de-gendering of sexuation?

Or course not, since *sexuation* includes and implies its own violation/difference or *(père-)version* as Lacan's graph of *sexuation* shows. Obviously homosexuals are governed by gender-rule—if not the very expression would not make any sense. It is not a sexual identity but a version of the same; a variation on the same theme. Hegel wrote that unity carries dualism, duality or contradictions within it, via the different principles that classical logic call *ex-toto*, *ex-nihilo*, and *ex-separato*. 1 is opposed to 2, then becomes 2, in order to be reborn as 3 in dialectics. 2 makes1in dialogics (via what is called *separato*) that is to say that a new unit is formed from that from which it is separated.

What is important to remember is that the whole functions in such a way that it is present within every one of its parts. The whole is based on the parts, which, likewise, reversing the courtesy, are based on the whole. There is a hologrammatic principle in human civilizations which expresses itself through structures, and which forces the parts constituting the whole to always function in such a way that the whole is contained /present within every one of its parts—something identity politics has a tendency to forget. That is to say that under the sun of the phallus, on the *sexuation* divide, one does not escape the unifying, universal law by which the two genders and their "*père-version*"/diversion/inversion are but the products of a process and become producers of a process that produces them, from which one does not escape, unless one annihilates the object of desire/*jouissance* and falls into the pure *jouissance* of the Big Other (God) such as do Medieval recluses, monks or nuns, yogis, holy men, etc.

Wo/men/cultures are defined by their attempts at escaping the laws of nature. Sexuality is already an unconscious way of escaping the laws of nature. Progress and emancipation imply a certain calculated way of trying to escape nature... But are the attempts at escaping the laws of *sexuation* genuine crossings of foundational forms' barriers? Of "subjectified substances"?

One fantasizes that one can escape gender-definition and the phallic function and destiny, (what Deleuze calls the subordination of the becoming of humans to the logic of the genus which is directly linked to the destiny of the family—an oppressive and reactionary defect which, for Deleuze and Guattari , characterizes and limits normative Freudian psychoanalysis), and there is nothing wrong with this, as long as one does not believe that the moon is made of green cheese, i.e. that by letting one's identity fall in an LBGTQ+ category, one becomes a self-made wo/man... By the same token, trying to impose the choice of new pronouns on the human collectivity or socius (it/their/them/zer...) as a better fit for one's body/desire, is but an empty gesture; it is more like whipping the surface of a pond in order to make consequential ripples than a genuinely creative gesture such as the process of swirling turbulences that create the stars, matter and so on....

Queer feminists would then reply, that the whole task is to destroy the law of the phallic signifier as foundational signifier of desire—something that feminists have tried to do for decades, as Joan Copjec shows in her seminal book *Read My Desire*.

But beyond this destruction of male/female normative sexuality, two correlated, more or less hidden objectives exist. One is the destruction of the other sex:

> *"The height of sexism is to regard the other sex as a different race. This is the objective of 'hard' feminism: a world expurgated of the male race. This is the same, though opposite, as happens in* Il mondo senza donne. *The same eradication of the other on a homosexual basis, or a sisterly basis, a basis of twinship or incest.*
>
> *The other tendency is, rather, to supplant men in positions of power. The male position being virtually unoccupied (since man has virtually disappeared), the feminists are in an enormous hurry to move into it, and they naturally fall into the trap that is the void of power itself. In the same way, political power being emptied of its substance, the Left rushed to seize it and immediately disintegrated in the void."*[8]

The other implies that the incest taboo would have to be abolished in order to destroy any constraints/restrains on sex and to bend gender until it breaks—which may signify the end of desire. The ultimate escape from gender-rule and so-called sexual exploitation/oppression implies the abolition of the incest-taboo (something most queer theorists refuse to even acknowledge).

Biologists' Mistake

For biologists, human sexuality is a functional, animalistic condition, the product of the environment and evolution, obeying instinctual and normative laws geared towards the reproduction of the species. Sexuality obeys electro-chemical impulses generated in the brain (cognitivism) and follows genetic program-like imprints in a deterministic mode. This type of positivist explanation privilege purely materialist conceptions of the body as given/imposed by nature (strangely following a re-vamped Cartesian dualism). Its avatars such as physical essentialism, empiricism (scientific tools allow the collection/gathering of data—Masters and Johnson; The Kinsey Report...), experiential and behavioral psychology, evolutionary biology.., all forego any cultural and/or psychoanalytical explanations/interpretations. For them nature predominates over culture, although social, civil, and legal norms maintain and regulate these innate, natural functions. According to this interpretation which wants to pass as absolute (science-based), deviations (homosexuality for instance) are seen as generated in the brain or even the result of a different coding of the genome, or the result of hierarchical, dominance-based behavior (some scientists speak of "the homosexuality gene," while others speak of homosexual behavior in societies of primates.) Many biologists, brain-specialists, and human scientists, believe that human sexuality obeys normative/regulative functions exercising their power from an extraneous position (inherent to the body but outside of consciousness) and making their laws felt in the field of daily life where their power is applied: causality runs from body to mind, and from sex to gender.

Curiously enough, although racism is a metonymic naturalization/essentialization of physical differences, many homosexuals often prefer a biological explanation for the origin of sexual desire:

> *"The strange assent among homosexuals to their being defined genetically. They prefer their difference to be biologically legalized. In the end, everyone prefers genes as the perfect alibi. The unconscious served in time as universal justification. But that was still a psychical agency. Now it is biology that is becoming the juridical guarantee, the basis of legal argument. Difference, positive or negative, is being embodied in an immanent reason. Gene biology and sociobiology seem to have a bright future ahead of them."*[9]

The Historicists or American Foucauldians' mistake

The origin of the mistake is based on their belief that human sexuality does not obey any given or pre-ordained/pre-determinate laws, or even a pre-determined reality re-enforcing itself via language. Sex is not theorized or privileged as an outside which pre-exists culture, i.e. the normative (bodies must occupy their proper places—hence the repressive dimension of normative sex enforced by a particular society), and the operations of power guaranteeing a certain accepted sexual behavior, what queer theorists call the hegemony (dominance, repression and oppression) of heterosexuality. Foucault, contrary to biologists, cognitivists, and human scientists, believed that sex is not only immanent, but also mutually interdependent with norms. For him, it is an "at once produced and producing process," following a constant back-and-forth movement between cause and effect, like Escher's hand drawing itself. For Foucault, sex is descriptive and discursive, normative and speculative, producing its own practices while subverting its own rules and norms. One can understand why queer theorists (Butler for instance) followed Foucault blindly, since sexual behavior can escape the assignment/consignment of sex to/by, gender's normativity. Their mutual interdependence can be pried open by counter-cultural moves, militancy, rebellious sexual activities and practices... Sexual freedom means, here, the freedom of choosing one's way and partner with whom one chose to orgasm (pleasure principle), and becomes the result of a revolutionary practice, in the same way as class-domination revolution—or so it is believed.

The American Foucauldians adduced an idealism of sexual production/behavior based on choice and creativeness (curiously enough in synch with what neo-capitalism and consumerism proposes). One chooses or invents one's gender and one's object of choice at will—the sky is the limit: homo or hetero-sex with different partners of the same or other sex, sex with objects, with animals. Some people even go as far as marrying objects, monuments, or their pets, although the champions of free sexual choice have the tendency to privilege homosexuality.

American application of Historicism and Foucauldianism: Butler's Performativeness.

Judith Butler's intelligent and informed theorizing has a direct practical, political, and militant agenda, exposing the artificial, proscribed, and performative nature of gender identity by throwing stones and pebbles into the apparently calm and natural surface of sexual certitude. She "disturbs gender" (*Gender Troubles*) and challenges the "sexual status quo" to induce political progress for the rights of marginalized, gay, and lesbian identities.

Butler wants to change people's minds about sexual identities by de-essentializing these identities. Following Simone de Beauvoir's existential view of feminineness (one is not born a woman, one becomes one) and, influenced by Althusser's notions of cultural hegemony (he himself borrowed from Gramsci), of over-determination (he borrowed from psychoanalysis), and Ideological and State Apparatuses, Butler de-natures the belief that gender is nature-given. She shows that gendered behavior (associated with femininity/ masculinity) is an act, a performance, a construction imposed upon us all by hegemonic, normative heterosexuality. Here Butler is directly influenced by the British psychoanalyst Joan Riviere's "*Womanliness as a Masquerade*," an essay analyzing the sexual feminine as a defensive mask put on to hide masculinity.

Riviere's feminineness or "*masquerade*" also influenced Lacan's Imaginary and Symbolic "feminine sexual attitude." Butler and late 20th century's feminists and film theory critics appropriated (while changing its intention) Riviere's "feminine performative" to de-essentialize and deconstruct gender: we are not our "bodies." We merely "act and pretend" to be our bodies as if on a stage (Shakespearean "*the world is a stage*") by following a prescribed script imposed on us via culture and education (Althusser's Ideological Apparatuses). In order to de-construct gender's imposition, Butler claim that people are not self-governing agents but are subjectified and reified by "*constituting acts..., constituting the identity of the actor*...[and] *constituting that identity as a compelling illusion, an object of belief*." But, Butler also questions "sexual idealist constructivists'self-assurance" because she doubts the extent to which "free," "self-choosing" individuals can change and constitute new sexual identities (as in theatrical acting). She consequently investigates the extent to which humans' sexual identity is determined by (or co-valent with) their place within culture: language, conventions, taboo.

Butler follows poststructuralist practice in using the term "subject" (rather than "individual" or "person") in order to underline the linguistic nature of our subjective positioning within what Jacques Lacan calls the Symbolic order (system of signs and conventions over-determining our perception of reality). She argues that the very daily routine-act of "gender performance" constitutes our sexual identity, **and nothing else**: sexual identity is an illusion retroactively created by our performances: there is no gendered self prior to its acts. Like the existentialists (de Beauvoir), Butler thinks that existence precedes essence. She believes that, retroactively, the repetitive performance of an imposed sexual identity (education, training...), re-enforced and compelled by social sanction and taboos as well as subtle and obvious coercion, convinces human beings that "sexual identity" is nature-given.

Following Foucault and borrowing from Kristeva, Butler also concludes that this cultural, sexual normativity and exclusivity creates a disgusting "otherness" and intolerable difference: "*a domain of unthinkable, abject, unlivable bodies.*" In a quasi-Zizekian move, Butler thinks that abjection is used by the normally/normatively obedient or docile subject to constitute him/herself as such via rejection/exclusion: "*This zone of uninhabitability will constitute the defining limit of the subject's domain; it will constitute that site of dreaded identification against, which—and by virtue of which—the domain of the subject will circumscribe its own claim to autonomy and to life.*" This "quasi -organic" or phobic repudiation is necessary for the subject to establish "*an identification with the normative phantasm of 'sex.'*" Butler, in a very feminist move (influenced by Julia Kristeva and Hélène Cixous' feminism) uses that concept of "abjected zone" (which, according to Kristeva, is sub-liminal—i.e. a liminality between consciousness and the unconscious) to "*rearticulate the very terms of symbolic legitimacy and intelligibility.*" She even goes farther by declaring that gender, as an objective, natural thing, does not exist: "*Gender reality is performative which means, quite simply, that it is real only to the extent that it is performed.*" Gender, according to Butler, is by no means tied to material bodily facts but is solely and completely a social construction, a fiction, one that, therefore, is open to change and contestation: "*Because there is neither an 'essence' that gender expresses or externalizes nor an objective ideal to which gender aspires; because gender is not a fact, the various acts of gender create the idea of gender, and without those acts, there would be no gender at all. Gender is, thus, a construction that regularly conceals its genesis.*" So far so good, except that Butler negates or forgets structure, incest taboo, the Mirror Stage, the unconscious, the Oedipus and Electra complexes...

Gender is concealed because of *sexuation* and cannot be unveiled discursively. But because of her agenda, Butler is persuaded (and wants to persuade others) that sexual genesis is only performative and that the body becomes its gender only "*through a series of acts which are renewed, revised, and consolidated through time.*" Using gender-construction's artificial/conventional/historical dimension as a machine-de-guerre, Butler attempts to destroy normative heterosexuality's assumptions: those "punitive" social/familial/legal rules forcing us to conform to hegemonic, heterosexual standards for identity. Butler nearly believes that homosexuality would reign if it were not for "heterosexual fascism."

Lacanian theory had already problematizes gender and sex by stating that there is a structural imbalance between the male and the female sides of *sexuation*, the "*all*" and the "*not-all*," because there is only one signifier to cover the lack (and absence) of the repressed primary object of desire: the m(o)ther. The phallus as "signifier of the lack" covers the primary object (the m(o)ther) for the male side of *sexuation*, expressing his desire on the one hand (the *all*). On the other hand, i.e. on the female side of *sexuation*, the other (or binary) signifier which would cover the primary object, (the m(o)ther), is missing. Lacan calls it the "*not all*," since this "lack of a lack" does not express in a complete or satisfying fashion the female lack (hence the expression *not-all*)—even if women opt for the "phallic signifier of the lack" attached to generally a male body, (or even a female body—and many do!).

Women's acceptance of the phallus as "signifier of the lack" to "signify their own lack" corresponds to what Joan Rivière calls "*the masquerade.*" In a compensatory move, culture tries to re-cover a unity and bridge the sexual gap and dissymmetry by trying to provide a symmetrical, signifying dyad or couple for sexual difference. But the binary signifier always lacks. It is fraught with troubling lack. The coupling does not couple well for the couple. It is often felt as a yoke by the female partner.

Well, is this postmodern, consumerist proliferation of genders and sexual identities not a desperate, quasi-agonized way for culture to attempt to compensate for the lack inscribed in the foundational gender bridge supposed to stand for sexual difference? In our contemporaneity this lack more and more provokes feelings of strong ambivalence, if not rage. It is as if, today, the "trouble with gender," and gender problems had become unbearable. Gender's lack of coherence induces incoherence and inchoate reasoning. It is seen as a primary and scandalous affront to selfhood and egotism—hence the various sexual identity politics.

Butler takes her formulations even further by questioning the very distinction between gender and sex. In the sixties and seventies, feminists regularly made a distinction between bodily sex (the *corporeal* facts of our existence) and gender (the *social* conventions that determine the differences between masculinity and femininity). Many feminists accepted the fact that anatomical differences do exist between men and women; but they were also quick to denounce the fact that the conventions that determine men's and women's behaviors are psycho-social/cultural constructions that do not have much to do with genuine corporeal advantages or disadvantages based on sexual differences. It is of course true that the belief in gender-based physiological and psychological differences has been used, throughout history, to limit and straightjacket women into roles and categories via material re-ification and "naturalization/essentialization" of/on/in the female bodies, and cultural propaganda/norms (what is now called sexism). For many feminists sex is a biological category, while gender is a cultural historical category (hence the label "historicists" given to them by feminist Lacanians). Following the postmodern continental thinkers and critics of the 70s and 80s, Butler, as she put it in *Bodies*, sex is an idealist construct materialized through time via the heterosexual, patriarchal hegemony and power-structure. She writes: sex is *"like a fiction, perhaps a fantasy, retroactively installed at a prelinguistic site to which there is no direct access."* Butler would be totally right, if it were not for the fact that there is a linguistic dimension which not only underlines/underwrites sex, but, also, is not accessible through linguistic consciousness because of the foundational repression of desire for/of the m(o)ther. This incest taboo prevents/obfuscates conscious choice. Nonetheless, as she adds, this sexual fiction is central to the establishment of subjectivity and human society, which is to say that, even so, it has material effects: "*the 'I' neither precedes nor follows the process of this gendering, but emerges only within and as the matrix of gender relations themselves*." Here Butler is right, although the "I," as well as desire, emerges after the sublation/repression of/for the m(o)ther desire. Since, as Lacan has shown, this linguistic construction, injunction, and imperative is not too stable, it needs constant re-enforcement: myths and foundational narratives, as Lévi-Strauss' sentence "*Il faut des rites*" epitomizes and explains—hence the cruel *sexuation* rituals and practices, laws, rules, taboos and regulations ... In order to re-establish boundaries, these "foundational stories" ground the repetitive performative acts that mark us as one sex or another, with the help of abjection (Julia Kristeva). What Butler forgets to ad is that "sex" is unveiled not only as an artificial norm but, in the same move, it is also re-veiled as such. Like the phallus (signifier of the lack), which, in order to "work," has to be veiled, sex can only work under cover. If there are no artifice, there is no sex. Sex is not conscious of its own genesis.

Contrary to what Butler argues, sexual normativity has a very limited latency for play or change; it is not really subject to change, unless one suppresses the incest taboo and if one opens up all the bodily orifices to the notion of penetration and exploration (something alluded to in Monique Wittig's *Le Corps Lesbien* (*The Lesbian Body*) where the lover's gaze makes love to her partner's body from the inside through a sort of bodily invagination (in Wittig's novel, both lovers are women). This spectral/specular love-making abolishing the inside/outside barrier is something that only women's *jouissance* (as "*Not-All*") can accomplish since it can relate to the signifier of the Other; it is not limited by the "*All*" of phallic *jouissance*. A man, in order to do the same thing as Wittig's lover, would have to have no access to the "*All*"–that is to be a psychotic.

The problem with such an "amorous move" is that it turns depth into a surface, bringing it up to the outside in order to be penetrated by the gaze, body-parts and objects of introspection. This internalization and penetration of the outside gaze is, by the way, the foundational principle of modern medicine, as Foucault explained in *The Birth of the Clinic*. This medical gaze is autonomized and takes on the fetish-like quality of partial objects such as scalpel, hands and gaze. They function in unison in order to bring the bodily depth to the surface, as if skin and inside-flesh form a sort of continuous, twisted ribbon (à la J.F. Lyotard with his "*grand ephemeral pellicle/skin*" concept) strangely similar in many aspects to the Mobius loop used by Lacan's clinical pedagogy to visualize the consciousness-language-unconscious continuity and rupture.

Butler's project as well as the LBGTQ+'s intentions of deconstructing/destroying binary genders, while exposing the heterosexual matrix by citing the arbitrariness of sexual binary-laws in order to displace the effect of its necessity, fall short of their intended agenda, which is ultimate liberation.

If generalized, these practices will end up de-genitalizing sex and privileging any surface or turning depth into an outside surface available for/suitable to the projection of desire (from body skin to car body). As with the Transformer Toys, the inside/outside opposition is turned into a surface streamlined for the imposition/application of the flow of the continuous morphing of desire operated by neo-capital, bringing surplus-value on par with surplus-enjoyment (*jouissance*). [10]

Zizek, quoting Lecercle, is right on target and on the money:

> *"Normalcy starts to lose its hold. The regularities start to loosen. This loosening of normalcy is part of capitalism's dynamic. It's not a simple liberation. It's capitalism's own form of power. It's no longer disciplinary institutional power that defines everything, it's capitalisms' power to produce variety—because markets get saturated. Produce variety and you produce a niche market. The oddest of affective tendencies are okay—as long as they pay. Capitalism starts intensifying or diversifying affect, but only in order to extract surplus-value. It hijack affect in order to intensify profit potential. It literally valorizes affect. The capitalist logic of surplus-value production starts to take over the relational field of resistance to identity and predictable paths."* [11]

What the two preceding speculative tendencies of biological

sex and performative sex seem to conveniently (?) forget or decidedly ignore is four main facts obeying two directional fluxes: language and the unconscious.

a) Language exists before babies: humans are born into a world of language predating their birth (names, family culture and structures, etc.) and it takes at least 5 years of daily practice via total immersion before one is able to master key linguistic concepts automatically. One is born into a (family/social) narrative one tries to adopt, modify, makes one's own, use as spring-board, or as a guillotine...

b) Generally humans do not make love (or mate to use the poor words chosen by cognitivists and evolutionary biologists) to their siblings/ parents, etc. The laws of marriage and intermarriage have been strictly codified by culture in a diachronic and synchronic mode (Lévi-Strauss and Co.).

c) These marriage laws and behavioral gender-codes are the results of the foundational incest-taboo which rests at the origin of the culture/nature divide typical of humanity. The incest taboo is universal and without exceptions—except for the Gods, or God-like individuals (The Pharaohs).

d) These aforementioned facts have induced/favored in the human psyche and mind, an unprecedented development of the fantasy-dimension (what Lacan calls the Imaginary) based on the "unknown reality" of the unconscious (direct by-product of the incest taboo). That is to say that one does not make love to the other without passing by an Other, or what takes its place, informed/deformed/reformed/perverted/inverted/diverted... by one's desire and fantasies. The one who wants to be absorbed by, or absorb, a two, always goes through a three. The body of our desire is not necessarily the actual body of the other: it can be his/her body, his/her fantasized body, the body of another while making love to "one's usual other." One can also make love to the imagined/fantasized body of what one thought/imagined our mother or father wanted: the fantazised, unconscious image-body of the father's or mother's desire which then can correspond to the same body-gender as one's own (homosexuality)—something reduplicated in male homosexuality by the refusal of the boy's symbolic castration by the father, or the refusal of the symbolic seduction by the father in the case of lesbianism. This inter-relation, or attempt at, is always governed by an absent/present dimension of the fantasmatic body, of impossible body of the primeval other, which Freud calls "*Das Ding*." This repressed presence/absence is itself re-configurated by the Law, the interjection/interdiction of the Big Other (the *name-of-the-father*), i.e. the other (we should write the *f(O)ther*), of the primeval, maternal other (lost object of unicity and primary identity) whose presence and dimension forbids the fusion with, or return to the m(o) ther. One makes love with one's mind via one's body through a third instance, which can be the body or the (hyper-virtual) image of another, or mental, fantasy picture or another—something commodification and commercialism has known to capitalize upon for maximum profit. In sex the loop mind/body is primary and always implies an absent but secretly present Other (unconscious). This is why Lacan says that between the human sexes, the sexual relation does not exist, but *ex-sists*. Its laws have been written somewhere else by someone else (the Other of the unconscious), producing unconscious sexual structures—what Lacan calls *sexuation*.

Endnotes

1 This article is dedicated to the nomad/homeless intellectual Biodun Iginla, ex-director of the University of Minnesota Press, who experienced "gender troubles" by using the woman bathroom in the *Break Expresso* café, Spring 2013, in downtown Missoula, Montana. He received a police citation and became persona non grata at the café.

2 *If you say what you like, you will hear what you don't like.* (Terence in *Andria*, *Phormio*, and *Eunnuchus*; quoted by Saint Jérôme in *Against Rufinus.*). That is to say, one has to take responsibility for the construction of the message one sends and the meanings which may be thereof enclosed (although one cannot be responsible for or foreclosed meaning), for, as Lacan said in the famous Seminar on *The Purloined Letter* (in *The Purloined Poe*. Baltimore: The Johns Hopkins University Press, 1988), a letter always arrives at its destination.

3 University of Montana Newspaper, *Montana Kaimin* Volume CXVI. Issue 36. *Transitions in a world of uncertainty: transgender conference highlights health care* (Madelyn Beck).

4 Lacan. *Séminaire 20: Encore.* Seuil: Paris, 1975. Two Sessions were translated by Jacqueline Rose in *Feminine Sexuality.*

5 Jean Baudrillard. *Fragments: Cool Memories II, 1990-1995.* Verso: London, 1997. 141

6 Mimi Marinucci. *Feminism is Queer: The Intimate Connection between Queer and Feminist Theory*. London: Zed Books: London, 2010. 234

7 Jean Baudrillard. *Politics: A Plea for Cultural Revolution in Organ Without Bodies: On Deleuze and Consequences*. Routledge: London, 2004. 183, 184.

8 Jean Baudrillard. *Fragments: Cool Memories II, 1990-1995.* Verso: London, 1997. 117

9 Jean Baudrillard. *Fragments: Cool Memories II, 1990-1995.* Verso: London, 1997. 95, 96

10 Michel Valentin. *The Centennial Review.* Winter 1992. Volume XXXVI No. 2. 1992.

11 Brian Massumi. *Navigating Moments* in *Hope*, edited by Mary Zournazi. Routledge: New-York, 2002. 224

Violence, Creativity, and the Unconscious of Nature

Robert S. Corrington, PhD

Introduction

The argument of this essay is perhaps a strange one. I am persuaded that there is a deep inner connection between violence and creativity in the human process and that both are rooted in the unconscious of nature. First, a definition of terms is in order. By "violence" I mean the shattering of form that may or may not be redeemable. While violence permeates our Darwinian universe, my focus will be on what human beings do, both personally and collectively, to shatter legitimate form (or gestalts). This overthrow of gestalts is rooted in nature and has a deep evolutionary history. In our species, it has taken on an extra fold, as it were, and can easily enter the slippery slope toward genocide.

For most, creativity is the antipode to violence. Here, I am defining "creativity" as the deep struggle to transfigure what violence does into a new "gestalt of grace" (Tillich), especially in the realms of science, the arts, and in the structure of the personality (psyche). The artist especially has a dual task; namely, to generate, often through an immense struggle, complex and rich products that are of value to the community, and to remake her or his psyche into a more fully individuated being. I refer to this latter aspect as the "Selving process," about which more will be said.

Harder to define is the "unconscious of nature." Clearly, most can accept the existence of a personal unconscious, some of whom can also accept the notion of a collective (species wide) unconscious in Jung's sense. For those of us who accept the reality of the human collective unconscious, it is still a huge leap toward the idea that *nature* has an unconscious dimension. But a key distinction can carry us forward toward an affirmation of this belief in the depth and abyss of nature. I refer to the ancient distinction (seen in Averroes, Aquinas, and later in Spinoza) between *natura naturans* (nature naturing) and *natura naturata* (nature natured). I define nature naturing as: "Nature perennially creating itself out of itself alone." The focus is on the creating, not on a creator, while the temporal sense shifts from "infinity" to "perennially," to denote that there is not an infinite time, but rather a cyclical process of self-renewal. A good analogue to my use of this notion is that of Schopenhauer's central concept of the Will (*der Wille*). For Schopenhauer, the Will is but an endless blind churning that has no teleology and isn't even conscious of itself as Will. It is truly opaque, as is nature naturing.

I define nature natured as: "The innumerable orders of the World." These orders are innumerable because they simply can't be counted, even by an alleged divine mind. The World's orders have no contour, no inner verses outer boundary, and are endlessly complex. There is no super order or "organism of organisms" (Whitehead) that could serve as a container for all that prevails. Further, this complexity entails that there are no simples. Even an alleged "simple" would have to be located somewhere and thus have relational traits. I will attempt to exhibit phenomenologically the multi-faceted relationships between nature naturing and nature natured.

Violence

It is my contention that violence is hard wired into our evolutionary heritage (Zoja) and that it is not simply a product of learned behavior. It is who we are as a species; namely, a predatory creature that turns on its own with waves of massive violence in which millions have died, and presumably will continue to do so. As noted, violence is the shattering of what I will call "legitimate" form, that is, gestalts that enrich the individual and the community. Obviously, this entails that some gestalts are destructive and what Kant would call "heteronomous." These latter forms are shattering in themselves in that they already impose an alien norm onto the self and its communities that are struggling for autonomy. The individual belongs to many communities at once, but in different respects. Some of these communities are consciously affirmed and may have been solidified by a public oath, while many others are but dimly known at all, and there are even communities to which the individual belongs, but is totally unconscious of doing so until some crucial event opens their eyes. A prime example is that of white racism. Rarely will someone label themselves as a racist, thus signaling a pathology in the psyche of those who do, while for many of us, we are racists under the skin, as it were. Suddenly there may come an awakening that one was a racist all along, but with an unconscious denial of the fact, combined with the fact of white privilege providing many seen and unseen advantages. Clearly, this argument applies to sexism and other forms of the projection of Otherness.

But what triggers violence in the first place? In his brilliant book, *Paranoia: The Madness that Makes History*, Jungian analysist and historian Luigi Zoja, traces violence back to the ubiquitous presence of paranoia. How does his argument work? The first thing he notes is that paranoia often starts with a special "revelation" that is deeply tribal in its core. Revelations, so-called, are simply not subject to self-critique, especially insofar as they seem to have a divine origin. Revelations are "anti-psychological" in that they block any probing of the psyche by the psyche. As beyond critique they cannot be questioned by the community that becomes infected by one (and they often come in a self-reinforcing series). Wilhelm Reich refers to this process of infection as the "emotional plague" that ripples through the unconscious of a community at blinding speed. There may be no cure for it unless strong social psychological forces and analyses are brought into play. But this is rare given the power of a paranoid plague.

Freud's ground breaking work should not be ignored. While I am much friendlier to Jung, and reject Freud's patriarchal and paternalistic perspective, he did show the link between violence and in-born aggression, thus adding more heft to Zoja's views. One of Freud's key texts on this issue is *Civilization and Its Discontents* (1930). One can only adumbrate it in the briefest terms. The basic argument is well known; namely, that humans are distinct among the animals in having created civilization. Yet this ongoing creativity comes at a high price. The sublimation of the erotic drive makes art and other creative products possible, but the frustration caused by sublimation can be deepened by the need of the society for order, cleanliness, and control. We each become our own Führer principle through the super-ego that is what Hegel would call, "the spirit of negation." At some point, this instinctual frustration boils over into aggression toward the Other.

Repressed instincts turn into aggression and guilt caused by the internal policing of the super-ego. A frustrated libido turns into neùrotic symptoms. The civilized social grouping frustrates libido on a *grand* scale and diverts it into a sense of communal identity, which can lower unconscious anxiety. However, as noted, no homogenous and heteronomous community can be imposed via the Führer principle without at the same time demonizing the Other. In addition to close neighborly ties, the worm can quickly turn on these same neighbors. ". . . their neighbor is for them not only a potential helper or sexual object, but also someone who temps them to satisfy their aggressiveness on him, to exploit his capacity for work without compensation [slavery], to use him sexually without his consent, to seize his possessions, to humiliate him, to cause him pain, to torture and to kill him." (pg. 111). This process includes violence and aggressiveness toward the Earth itself. In his recent lengthy article, *The Uninhabitable Earth*, David Wallace-Wella argues that the latest scientific evidence on global warming points to very rapid global warming and gives our species about 150 years to live. In this sense, Freud had it right, that our aggressive instincts have decimated not only whole human populations through genocide, but has also turned against the biosphere that makes life possible.

Linking this back to Zoja and others, Freud's aggressive instinct could not flourish without the presence of personal and communal paranoia. The first thing paranoia does is to create a fear of the posited Other. This fear starts out as unconscious at first but can be made conscious via a powerful leader. In paranoia, the path toward violence increases, as the individual and the associated community want a removal of the anxiety that this uneasy fear produces. Thus, following Heidegger, we can make a distinction between fear and anxiety, with the latter being somewhat vague and less localized. If fear is of a specific and known object, it can be dealt with by personal and/ or communal means. But anxiety, especially in its purer forms, becomes an opening into nothingness. It is impossible to "deal" with nothingness as if it can be converted to solid being.

The self can react to the perceived threat of nothingness in one of two extreme ways, always on a living continuum. The first, and more common, extreme is to recoil in horror because self-identity is threatened. The self feels as if it will become fragmented and bereft of a stable personality. This impending sense of the loss of identity, personal and tribal, compels the self to react violently in the other direction and to take on a new identity that comes from the so-called revelation that the leader has and who conveys this revelation to the community. This relationship of the "born again" self is directly tied to the Führer principle. For only an extreme leader can have the will to impose a new mythology onto the tribe and bring that tribe into heteronomous obedience. Being "born again," whether in a religious or secular context, is basically a pathological move to save identity at all costs, even that of killing the healthier self within.

At the other extreme, the self can welcome the liberating power of nothingness in its nihilating events, and more gently create a richer self-identity. But note, this remaking of the self is not due to a recoil motion that thrives on a dualism between: 1) the old and new self where the latter is a complete negation of the former, and 2) the special privileged self and its now demonized Other. The healthier self has no need to demonize the Other because it is not haunted by the Other within. For the paranoid and anxious self, it will constantly be reminded of its former *abjected* self and must become rigid to try and keep it at bay. Being "born again" makes one more of a captive than before the violent conversion under the Führer principle. With the opposite momentum toward an embracing of nothingness and the Encompassing (Jaspers), the new self can become free from the abjection of itself and other communities. This form of the new self utterly rejects heteronomous impositions from the leader and engages in social critique and the quest for liberation from demonic abjections.

Violence comes into the picture quickly within the 'revelation' driven community. One of the surest signs that a community is prone to violence is with how they view their sacred text(s). Of course, there can be secular sacred texts such as the writings of Marx for a shrinking part of the earth's population. The height of this madness comes when a community takes its chosen text literally. While there can be no such thing as a literal reading of anything, except perhaps the phone book, the illusion of literalism has a strong hold on people who have succumbed to the "emotional plague." The claim to a "literal" reading of a religious text boils down to a rigid interpretation imposed on the tribe by the Führer principle. The leader, almost always a male, is ultimately concerned with power and self-glorification, but is usually not aware of the fact. He sees himself as being "righteous" and, though a sinner, above the fray.

Thus, the link between literalism and violence is becoming clearer. If one has a chosen religious or secular text and then affirms that it is infallible and can only have one true interpretation, it follows that all other such texts must be heretical or even demonic. A battle between and among these texts and their 'literal' adherents, is inevitable, very often of genocidal proportions. Violence is a child of paranoia and becomes unleashed rather easily, even in a democracy. The paranoid stance is one that believes that there is a hostile Other who is ultimately bent on one's destruction. There is what Zoja calls a "slippery slope," mentioned above, that makes the downward trajectory to ultimate violence quite possible. Paranoia begets paranoia about the selected Other, who then, in turn, develops paranoia about the first group. This is the slippery slope, as "evidence" is easily compiled about the machinations of the Other and alternative facts suddenly emerge to totally darken the impulse toward truth. Each side accuses the other of having generated made up or alternative facts. Truth is always the victim in the violence prone paranoid mind.

Creativity

True and great creativity cannot exist without some antecedent violence that shatters the gestalt that the artist, in this case, is trying to transform into a newer and more enriched gestalt. In addition, the cultural creative can deliberately crack open established genre forms to clear the way for the above mentioned "gestalt of grace." Thus, violence can be either inherited or created fresh. My argument is that high creativity cannot get off the ground without some violence to invoke it into being. There is thus a strange alchemical marriage between violence and creativity. However, there are certain limits. Extreme violence usually blocks the path to inquiry and it is not uncommon for cultural creatives to be the objects of direct violence, either through imprisonment, banishment, or execution. The loss to the community is great.

I distinguish between "sterile or inert communities," and "communities of interpretation." The former type of community is one in which violence and paranoia keep vigilance against the emergence of novel signs and symbols. The inert community moves on a rectilinear trajectory that doesn't tolerate changes in direction or even novelty per se. No new interpretants (Peirce), that is, new signs, can enter public consciousness. A key example of this is the absurd notion that Darwinian evolutionary theory is somehow a *mere* theory and doesn't withstand the tests of biblical 'truth.' For the sane mind, the evidence for the truth of organic evolution is simply overwhelming, while for the pathological plague filled mind, genuine tested and replicated theories are reduced to the realm of fantasy. This pathology is one of the most dangerous in our era as it tends to further undermine scientific inquiry and the objective use of much abused reason.

Cultural creatives cannot function, except underground, in an inert community governed by the Führer principle. Their work is abjected and demonized, thus rendering creativity mute. The type of violence instantiated in the inert community is purely heteronomous and may not be redeemable. Anything radical or avant guard is quickly rendered under the category of the "degenerate," "secular," or "bourgeois." In its place, the tribe eulogizes propaganda and the purely banal. Thus, there is no real hope for cultural creativity in the inert communities.

However, the second form of community, the "community of interpreters," is a place where cultural creatives (geniuses) can flower and generate a rich tapestry of novel interpretants. Such a rarer community welcomes the admission of creative products that enhance personal and communal understanding of the Selving (individuation) process. In the Selving process, the self/psyche of the individual and that of its community, reach a higher level of intensity. New gestalts replace shattered forms with a radiance of more scope and power.

Selving involves the maximization of available potency within the psyche (personal and collective). It requires a high degree of self-consciousness of one's internal and external sign systems and their semantic meanings. Self-consciousness is not possible without meaning and formal hermeneutics can be a great aid in finding the regnant contours of meaning-fields, or horizons. Much effort has been devoted to the task of defining "consciousness" and whether other species have it in at least a minimalistic sense. The concern here is far more with that species within the genus consciousness we know as self-consciousness. Creativity is not possible without it and violence and paranoia can and do function without self-reflexivity. In fact, self-consciousness—the psyche probing itself—is a counter foil to the bland consciousness that goes with violence and paranoia. Simply put, the more self-consciousness there is, the less the likelihood there is of unconscious violence and the demonization of the Other.

What is a creative product and what is its relation to violence? Initially we can say that such an advanced product, be it in the arts or the sciences, wrestles with the ongoing disruption of form that ultimately comes from the abyss of nature. The cultural creative directly feels the shock waves of the breaking of form in the gestalts with which she or he is intimately concerned. These rude vibrations awaken a counter-response in the creative individual that aches for a generation of new form. Creatives almost always feel an uncontrollable longing for the sheer act of high level creation. When trained (or intuitive) talent is combined with genius, the impulse is to create a product within one or more genera or fields. Longing, fueled by an ache that won't go away, must generate a product to momentarily still that longing. Of course, there is no end to the process as one fulfilled longing leads to a further ache and longing and the will to create yet another product.

The product itself will be constituted by powerful gestalts of great scope and semiotic density. By "semiotic density" is meant that sign systems can fold in over themselves again and again. With each infolding meaning is enhanced and the product takes on more power of being. For the sensitive individual, and the relevant community of interpreters, meanings can ramify indefinitely, thereby one can affirm that any great created product can be probed, assimilated, and explored without end. This openness is the goad to query, which can be defined as "inventive wonder." Cultural creatives thus serve to bring deep levels of query into the Selving process, enhancing its ability to see wonder in all its forms, whether natural or humanly created.

The next step in the creative Selving process is to transition from the generation of violence-assimilating products to the more demanding process of creating a new psyche. The cultural creative must now treat the psyche as a work of art itself. This holds as well for the scientist whose theories may also have personal implications for creating a more capacious and wonder-filled self. Both scientists and artists, not to forget all other types, must struggle to bring a new contour of gestalts into their lives. This also entails a greater awareness of the violence that permeates the human species and of its potential creative uses. For example, one could argue that the Big Bang in astrophysics is known nature's single most violent act. Yet, all creativity emerged from that act as well. This violence continues on a cosmic scale, while creative transfigurations punctuate this larger state. Of course, the word "violence" here must be used with the proper semantic nuances to differentiate it from the "violence" of organic forms. But the main concern here is with how the Selving process makes the move from creative products to a self-created new psyche.

In my view, purpose is extremely rare in nature. It belongs to creatures with enough self-consciousness to *envision* a future state of new being. This emergent teleology can be highly creative for the persons well on the way to fulfilling the Selving process. However, for persons with only a minimal or even non-existent self-consciousness, purpose is imposed by the Führer principle in an inert community. Thus, it is not purpose or teleology at all, but a simple pre-determined trajectory not self-created by the community or individual. Purpose must be forged through creative will against the forces of inertia and bare continuity. When it does emerge, it brings about an ontological phase transition in the Selving process. This transition allows the future to become more open to the energies and forces of the past and present, while also refusing to rest on current or antecedent positions. The more open future, held open by the creative nihilating acts of nothingness, provides the room within which the psyche can find both its depth self and its even deeper link to the unconscious of nature.

The Uunconscious of Nature

We will start with the human unconscious and its two dimensions. The first dimension is, of course, the personal unconscious. It is largely generated by perceptions and events acquired during the person's life time. Much of it is accessible to memory, perhaps through hypnosis or psychoanalysis. Yet a large part of it will always remain unconscious in certain respects. It is a fool's errand that assumes that the personal unconscious can be rendered into lucid consciousness. For Jung, and for me, the personal unconscious contains what he called "feeling toned complexes." The language is precise here. A "complex" is a growing cluster of memories, intuitions, and analogous connections. It cannot be exhaustively rendered conscious by any known means. It has depths that are beyond the reach of the attending ego. The complex is "feeling toned" because it has highly charged affects that become manifest whenever it is encountered, especially when least expected. For example, suppose one has a deep mother complex. It is constituted by actual memories from infancy and beyond of the biological mother or care giver. In later adult life, many events or perceptions in the world or in dream life, have a family resemblance to the originating traits of the growing complex. Thus, a given encounter with a woman could trigger the original complex and that woman would be subject to the, perhaps, negative projections that come from the core of the complex. This could taint all such relations. Further, via analogy, an object could come to symbolize the other traits of the mother complex, such as a knife or a patch of blood.

Feeling toned complexes can be partially awakened through

technique, such as the word association test, but their shifting and growing content is never fully recoverable. What makes these personal unconscious complexes so powerful determinates of adult behavior and ideation? The answer lies in the collective unconscious that the person shares with the tribe and the species. The collective unconscious was never personal and never contains individual traits. It consists, not of complexes, but of archetypes that are part of phylogenetic inheritance. These archetypes were not acquired through the Lamarckian passing on of acquired traits, but are rooted in nature and its evolutionary momenta. Archetypes can evolve in the "infinite long run" (Peirce) and adapt to changing conditions, although at a glacial pace as is appropriate. What happens is that a personal unconscious complex becomes rooted in its corresponding archetype. Thus, a mother complex becomes embedded in the archetype of the Great Mother, who was the source for the oldest religion in species history and is still viable today.

The collective unconscious prevails before the split into what we mean by good and evil. This later distinction should not be imposed on the unconscious. What we have in the personal and collective unconscious is the above mentioned alchemical marriage between violence and creativity. It is up to the Selving process to move the violent traits of the unconscious (Jung's "shadow") toward and through the alembic of creativity. For Tillich, creativity always contains an element of the "demonic." The German Romantic tradition, from Beethoven to Thomas Mann, eulogized this relationship in rather strong terms. I would argue that the shadow is the threat of inner and outer heteronomy.

We have already made a phenomenological move into the depths of the collective unconscious. But, one might ask: how can phenomenology, as the science of the evident and the given, ever render something non-evident and non-present into phenomenological description? The answer comes through a transformation from transcendental or hermeneutic phenomenology to what I call an "ordinal" phenomenology. I created this new version of phenomenology precisely to move beyond the present and the evident into the deeper surrounding territory of the unconscious. There is a striking sense in which complexes and archetypes are certainly co-present and leave clear traces of their makeup and activities. One can learn the subtle process of 'seeing' them out of the corner of one's eye. The prefix "ordinal" refers to the notion that any complex or archetype has an ordinal location somewhere in human nature and in nature per se. Neither complexes or archetypes are non-located 'simples,' as there can be no such thing. Hence, they have deep and strong relational traits that vibrate through the psyche and nature. These traits can be rendered available to the carefully trained vision (not to forget the other senses).

In the final transition, we move toward the unconscious of nature, which is the ground and abyss for the collective and personal forms of the unconscious. This rootless abyss and ground is fissured, as noted, into nature naturing and nature natured. Nature naturing (*natura naturans*) is the term/eventing with priority. This is so because nature in its naturing is the ground and abyss for the ejection of archetypal Forms and the emanation of the orders of nature natured (*natura naturata*). Ejecting is a more violent movement to propel a potency into instantiation as a governing archetype. This process is perennial and self-renewing. Emanation is the gentler form of making manifest. There is no one emanation from the One, but a perennial series of emanations upon emanations that collectively form the orders of the world. The processes of ejection and emanation are without guile or reason, nor is the emitting source conscious of what 'it' does. The unconscious of nature, here equated with nature naturing, is an abyss without light or awareness, yet it is also the self-giving ground for what does prevail in whatever mode it does prevail.

Nature's unconscious is what makes both the collective and personal unconscious possible. It is my belief that consciousness emerges out of the unconscious of nature into its Selving process where the extra layer of self-consciousness can emerge, however fitfully, under the constraints of finitude. We can catch a real glimpse of these events through the ordinal lens of phenomenology, newly ground. One can 'see' and certainly feel the ejective potency of nature naturing once the right language is fashioned for these liminal experiences.

And one can feel the gentler emanations that lie in the inner propulsions of nature. Here Spinoza's word *conatus* comes to the fore. In *conatus* (striving toward more excellence of self-being) the dynamism of the orders of the world is manifest. This striving does not require or entail motion or change of place. In the unconscious of nature this striving is a central trait and our encounter with it, through our personal and collective unconscious, can be filled with the wonder that spawns query.

Finally, the unconscious of nature is the non-located location for the entwinement of violence and creativity. At a recent Congress at my university the theme was "Suffering and Evil in Nature." One would expect that the participants would easily slide into the 'obvious' distinction between suffering throughout nature and evil as confined to the human process. Yet some brave souls were willing to entertain the notion that evil was in non-human nature as well. It is to be noted that they were not speaking from a Christian framework in which nature is a fall from grace, but from a more philosophically neutral base. In pondering the notions of paranoia, violence, creativity, and the three dimensions of the unconscious, we have not raised the prospect that there could be something evil in nature. Schopenhauer came very close to this position from a decidedly atheistic perspective. I think that it is an issue worthy of our best philosophical and psychoanalytic efforts.

References and Bibliography

Buchler, Justus, *Metaphysics of Natural Complexes*, New York: Columbia University Press (1966), Second Expanded Edition, SUNY Press (1990), ed. Wallace, Marsoobian, and Corrington.

Canetti, Elias, *Crowds and Power*, trans. by Stewart, New York: Farrar, Straus, and Giroux (1962). German Edition (1960).

Corrington, Robert, *The Community of Interpreters*, Macon, GA: Mercer University Press (1987/1995).

Nature and Spirit: An Essay in Ecstatic Naturalism, New York: Fordham University Press (1992).

An Introduction to C.S. Peirce, Lanham, MD: Rowman & Littlefield Press (1993).

Ecstatic Naturalism: Signs of the World, Bloomington, IN: Indiana University Press (1994).

Nature's Self: Our Journey from Origin to Spirit, Lanham, MD: Rowman & Littlefield Press (1996).

Nature's Religion, Lanham, MD: Rowman & Littlefield Press (1997).

A Semiotic Theory of Theology and Philosophy, Cambridge: Cambridge University Press (2000).

Wilhelm Reich: Psychoanalyst and Radical Naturalist, New York: Farrar, Straus, and Giroux (2003).

Riding the Windhorse, Lanham, MD Hamilton Books (2003).

Nature's Sublime: An Essay in Aesthetic Naturalism, Lanham, MD: Lexington Books (2013).

Deep Pantheism: Toward a New Transcendentalism, Lanham, MD: Lexington Books (2016).

Nature and Nothingness: An Essay in Ordinal Phenomenology, Lanham, MD: Lexington Books (2017).

Freud Sigmund, *Civilization and its Discontents,* trans. by Strachey, in *Volume XXI of The Standard Edition of the Complete Psychological Works of Sigmund Freud,* London: The Hogarth Press, (1961). German Edition (1930).

Heidegger, Martin, *Being and Time,* trans. By Macquarrie and Robinson, New York: Harper & Row, (1962), German Edition (1927).

Introduction to Metaphysics, Second Edition, trans. by Fried and Polt, New Haven: Yale University Press (2014), German Edition (1935).

Jaspers, Karl, *Philosophy, Vol. 3,* trans. by Ashton, Chicago: University of Chicago Press (1971), German Edition (1932).

Jung, C.G., *The Archetypes and the Collective Unconscious, Second Edition, Vol. 9.1 of The Collected Works,* trans. by R.F.C. Hull, Princeton: Princeton University Press (1971), German Essays (1934-1950).

Kant, Immanuel, *Critique of the Power of Judgment,* trans. by Guyer and Matthews, Cambridge: Cambridge University Press (2000), German Edition (1793).

Lieberman, James E., *Acts of Will: The Life and Works of Otto Rank,* New York: Free Press (1985).

Peirce, C.S. *The Essential Peirce, Vol. 1 (1867-1893),* Bloomington, IN: Indiana University Press (1993).

The Essential Peirce, Vol. 2 (1893-1913), Bloomington, IN: Indiana University Press, (1998).

Rank, Otto, *The Trauma of Birth,* trans. by Lieberman, New York: Dover Publications, (1993), German Edition, (1924).

Art and Artist: Creative Urge and Personality Development, trans. by Atkinson, New York: W.W. Norton (1968), German Edition (1930).

Reich, Wilhelm, *Character Analysis*, trans, by Garfagno, New York: Farrar, Straus, and Giroux, (1972), German Edition (1933).

Robinson, Paul A., *The Freudian Left: Wilhelm Reich, Geza Roheim, Herbert Marcuse*, New York: Harper & Row, (1969).

Schopenhauer, Arthur, The World as Will and Presentation, Vol. 1, trans. by Aquila and Carus, New York: Pearson Longman, (2008). German Edition (1819).

Spinoza, Benedict de, *A Spinoza Reader*, trans. by Curley, Princeton: Princeton University Press, (1994). Latin Edition of *Ethics* (1677).

Tillich, Paul, *The Courage to Be*, New Haven: Yale University Press (1952).

Wallace-Wells, David, *The Uninhabitable Earth: Famine, Economic Collapse, A Sun that Cooks Us: What Climate Change Could Wreak—Sooner than You Think*, New York: New York Magazine, July 10, 2017.

Whitehead, Alford North, *Process and Reality: Corrected Edition*, New York: The Free Press (1978), Original Edition (1929).

Zoja, Luigi, *Violence: In History, Culture, and the Psyche*, trans. by Peck and Stirnimann, New Orleans: Spring Journal Books (2009), Italian Essays (2000-2008).

Paranoia: The Madness that Makes History, trans. by Hunt, Oxon, England, Routledge Press (2017), Italian Edition (2017).

'The House of Desolation' Felt Existential Psychoanalytic Approaches to Dasein-icide

Loray Daws, PhD

"My mother was like a vine—you know... those that grow over a pillar... and over time damages it... my mother was like that".

"Feels like a carpet burn on my soul"

"My soul has been seared"

Abstract

It will be the aim of the current paper to theoretically discuss, as well as clinically illustrate, various contemporary psychoanalytic and Dasein-psychoanalytic voices in understanding chronic interpersonal trauma referred to as Dasein-icide. This disenfranchised state experienced by various analysands opens up a dialogical space wherein a general 'absence' in the right to experience one's subjectivity as well as one's own affective states and perceptions seem evident. The Other as psychological guardian, protector, elucidator, enhancer, clarifier and scaffolder seems absent as understood by various developmental psychoanalysts. The concepts of cumulative trauma (M. Masud R. Khan), pathological accommodation (Bernard Brandchaft), soul murder (Leonard Shengold), and micro-trauma (M. Crastnopol) will be explored through literature, personal anecdotal reveries, as well as verbatim case material.

Introduction

The power of *dasein-icide* [1](DuBose, 2014) came to me, not only through clinical work, but as an awareness of how unknowingly it can present in daily being-with-others. I would thus like to start this paper with a personal anecdote. My son enthusiastically asked me to edit work that he was preparing for his class on Canadian history. At the time of this interaction my son was in grade 4, and as any enthusiastic 10-year-old, he wrote with much passion about his subject. His project was concerned with the coal miners of Northern BC in the late 1800s. In reading his work, I was taken by his sensitive interpretation of their sense of isolation, their pining for family, and their adaptation to various deprivations. He even ventured some moral dilemmas in that the need to find gold ultimately fostered greed and other forms of corruption of the soul. Given its importance, I approached the editing with a similar amount of enthusiasm, and wanted to ensure that he received a good grade. After my initial editing, having some concern that editing always seems, even on a PC, to be in red, I called him over for further editing. He again approached me with a buoyant look, made contact with his creation and "suddenly"[2] seemed to collapse. I could read in his face the impact of my work on his creation. He became quiet, tears welled up, and paradoxically in a voice filled with kindness[3] said to me: *"Dad, there is nothing of me left"*. I was taken aback by his reaction, experiencing a mix of self-awareness, shame, anger and confusion that this

1 I am deeply thankful to Prof DuBose for his concept of *Dasein-icide*. The use of Dasein borrows from Martin Heidegger and various Daseinanalysts to signify a way of being involved in one's immediate 'world'(-ing), a world (-ing) inhabited by an *autochthonous self* that continuously owns its awareness of facticity and the contingent elements inherent in self-world (-ing) involvement. To experience one's own Being, one's own (ed) truth (representing this unique world-'ing' as Soul) includes a continual Being –in, Being-for, and Being- with.

2 The work of Shengold (2011) comes to mind here

3 The incident in US—the Philando Castile shooting where a four year old tries to sooth a distraught mother.

had transpired between us—between my attempt to be helpful, and the impact it had on his own creation. Despite this moment of anguish, I turned to focusing on my agitation and feelings of shame as best I could, apologized and started reparation. I mentioned that my edits were not permanent and that we could undo them (if only we worked like Microsoft word!). I asked him to choose which edits he thought should remain, and that I would return the document to its original account. Out of a 30 minute editing task, he chose two words and seemed delighted by the changes. But most importantly, for me, he could let his dad's *dasein-icide* moment go. I experienced a deep sense of relief that he was not trapped with, or by me. He could move forward and I found his reaction and words deeply transformative and deeply relational—an **autochthonous** response to alterity.

The Concept of Cumulative Trauma

Moments of too-muchness, if not moments of not-enoughness, all possess the capacity to have a lasting impact on relational contexts and intrapsychic living. Although Freud may have been the most gifted clinician of our era, many works in philosophy, cosmology and theology write about man's desires and relational archetypes that both devastate and tantalize our shared human psychic equipment. Experiencing devastatingly tantalizing desires with, due, or in relation to the Other, as well as tantalizing devastation within ourselves and in relation to the Other, seems to serve as psychological soil for our greatest philosophers and poets[4]—culture's archetypal archivers. Freud's creative oeuvre articulated various such realities, and in now classical works (1915, 1920, 1923 & 1926) Freud maps various hypotheses wherein a lack of insulation sees the flooding of man's capacity. Similar to biblical floods, great damage can be created by a lack of a protective shield and only parts of the self may remain afloat or buoyant, able to, in time[5], resurrect and rebuild around traumatized (traumatizing)

4 Eigen's (1999) trauma statements: "(1) In the beginning there is nourishment; (2) in the beginning (almost) there is trauma, and (3) in the beginning there is nourishment-trauma." (p. 145). Eigen's work on Toxic Nourishment (1999) and Psychic Deadness (1995,1996) remains central to my clinical understanding of Dasein-icide and will be articulated in greater depth in a forthcoming publication (Daws, 2018, EPIS).

5 From Noah to Odysseus, surviving a catastrophe is but part of the

states of being. If we are so fortunate as to have good-enough environments (Winnicott, 1945, 1958, 1960, 1969, 1974), the so-called good-enough parents (being welcomed, having ontological security) (Laing, 1960), a tolerable cultural environment[6] as well as functioning biological equipment, many of us may survive and thrive within over- and under-stimulation. That is, if the stimulation-stress dialectic (stress equation) does not burden the native self excessively, the True Self or the *autochthonous drive* (Grotstein, 1997) remains largely saved/safe from excessive accommodation wherein the 'self' becomes largely an adaptational self[7]. Various 'adaptations' are possible—turning away from the Real and living as orphans (psychosis), living between rewarding and withdrawing paradigms of existence and walling off abandonment traumata (the so called borderline dilemma), living between inflation, deflation and a scarred sense of esteem (so called narcissism), negotiating master-slave or sadistic other and self-in-exile realities (so called schizoid compromise), to neurotic adaptations of control (obsessive compulsive), seduction (hysteria), distancing (paranoia), and many more. Even more insidious, and very relevant to the discussion to follow, are symptoms such as soul heaviness, soul fatigue and Sartre's soul ennui. Contemporary work, given nearly a century of observation as well as the extension of psychoanalytic parameters has also seen a greater *nuancing of trauma*—floods certainly do exist, but what to make of *lingchi* (Chinese for a death by a thousand cuts)? Many analysand describe nuanced interpersonal events that 'shock' them, shocks that repeat over time; "It was not like I was walking on egg-shells

---

task confronted. Returning home, if not re-finding a home remains beholden to temporality, wherein *time should be given time*. Contemporary soldiers frequently mention that modern warfare further traumatizes as overstimulation is not allowed an extended period of decompression, a time used exclusively for grieving. Rather, modern soldiers are frequently exposed to a process wherein, and within, a short period of time the psyche is exposed to an overstimulating environment/event to only shortly thereafter be thrust back 'into' an environment seen as 'normal'. This in itself may actually be too much to bear, exacerbating psychic traumata.

6 The absence of a *handicapper general* as described by Kurt Vonnegut (2010) in his short story *Harrison Bergeron*. This short story also emphases the opposite of psychic airbrushing as micro trauma as described by the psychoanalyst Crastnopol (2015).

7 I hope my psychoanalytic colleagues can forgive my reservation to use the term "False self" as cultural trends have appropriated Winnicott's beautiful description, and as such has subjected it to moral violence.

per se, although it did feel like it at times—it was more that I was trying to avoid min(d)efields!" Another analysand: "I am starting to 'see' my family. We were not beaten. It was *cumulative stresses of things that were not good*, not the extreme end of the scale, not the worst of it all, *but it's ongoing*.... I don't have enough words to describe it all accurately [as compared to an event/trauma]. I know now my mother didn't have the understanding to differentiate her own pain from our childhood, with how she treated us...."

With these various insights, analysands carry across valiantly the impact of *cumulative trauma* on the psyche, or in the insightful work of Margaret Crastnopol (2015), articulate the various micro-traumas that impact self functioning:

> "Injurious relating on the grossly abusive end of the scale is the time-honored stuff of history, fiction, drama, and contemporary psychoanalytic theory. But negative interactions that are evanescent can ultimately also have a strong psychic impact. Like sharp rocks only vaguely if at all visible beneath the water at the shore, such potentially damaging moments may go largely unregistered. As a result, these subtler occurrences, *especially in the aggregate*, can create psychic bruises that are hard to notice and harder to minister to, with the consequence that they *accumulate invisibly*. Such injuries can distort a person's character, undermine his or her sense of self-worth, and compromise his or her relatedness to others." (Crastnopol, 2015)(italics added).

A very articulate and interpersonally sensitive analysand (Tanya) mentions that although she spends time with her mother she experiences it out of a sense of duty rather than deep care and want. This makes her feel "like a horrible person". Over a weekend Tanya spontaneously decided to invite her mom along to the local nursery and coffee, as her mother loves nurseries. While extending the invitation Tanya's mom immediately negotiates changes and with much stress and fortitude Tanya remains resolute to follow her initial work rhythms. Since Tanya expected her mother to make comments Tanya took a further psychic leap and informed her husband (Kevin) concerning the various felt psychic impacts cultivated by her mother's snide remarks. Initially Tanya's husband seemed reluctant to 'see' the pattern ("a few snide remarks about me, under the guise of humour") but decided to keep an open mind;

> [Later the day]...I could tell by her body language that she was gearing up to make a snide remark toward me. I was telling Mom how I had a renewed interest in an activity, but how I misplaced the manual for my sewing machine. My mother's body language changed and she turned to Kevin and said in her snide, contemptuous but laughing way "You know my daughter always says that she rarely ever loses anything because she is quite organized at home, but it's not true, she can't even find the manual for her sewing machine (that by the way I had not used for 20 years)". Normally Kevin would agree and just laugh. Meanwhile I am feeling like it is all I can do to not burst out crying.
>
> It would be ridiculous to start to cry over my mother making a comment about me misplacing my sewing machine manual, and I totally get it. *But I can barely contain myself, and I recognize that it is not because of THIS comment, but the 10,000 comments that have occurred in my life time before this one.*
>
> But this time Kevin reached out, and put his arm around me and said; Actually she is pretty organized, and it must just be that she is just hanging out with me so much that she can't find things'.
>
> I think my mother was stunned. She said something like, "silly me, I guess that wasn't the nicest thing to say" I didn't say anything and was clearly not impressed by her comment. And that was the end of that.
>
> It didn't stop her though, as she managed to get another couple of snide comments in that had less of a bite for me."

Returning to the psychoanalytic concept of *dasein-icide* Masud Kahn gives a detailed overview in a paper entitled "The Concept of Cumulative Trauma"[8] of the various phases of Freudian and

8 Khan refers throughout his debate to the most prevalent paradigmatic traumatic situations archived to that point in clinical psychoanalysis

psychoanalytic thinking wherein the inner world is thought to adapt to the pressures and impingements emanating from the 'human environment'. These pressures and impingements could be categorized as parental neglect, abandonment or seduction; to inner thoughts, images and feelings that either traumatize or continue to haunt the self, foreclosing a sense of inner harmony. Clinical concepts such as the repetition compulsion, inter-systemic trauma; and the ego destroying superego attest to such strains and conflicts.

Immersed in the language of both Freud and his mentor Donald W. Winnicott, Khan set his sights on the function of the mother as protective shield and insulating presence, where contact with the outer world sees the creation of both an awareness of stimuli coming from the inside and outside 'worlds'. This insulation protects the budding self and concomitant ego functions, if you will, from flooding and traumatic entropy, accommodative strategies, if not from precocious adaptation. The latter is masterfully articulated by clinical psychoanalysts Michael Eigen (1977, 1981, 1983, 1985, 1986, 1993, 1995,1996, 1999, 2001, 2004, 2007) and Wilfred Bion (1957, 1958, 1959) and they continuously state in their work that *developing the apparatus to 'have' experiences for thinking and feeling* remain a lifelong task. Schematically Khan argues that Freud set out to articulate that 'contact' with the outer world, sees the creation of a "crust" and eventually a "protective shield." It is important to read that Freud himself postulated that "*Protection against* stimuli is almost more important function for the living organism than *reception* of stimuli. The protective shield is supplied with its own store of energy and must above all endeavour to *preserve* the special modes of transformation of energy operating in it against the effects threated by the *enormous energies at work in the external world*" (Freud, 1920, p. 27, cited in Khan, 1963, p. 289)(italics added).

It is evident, given the many cases described by Freud, that parental seduction (over excitement/flooding) served as bedrock to the shock trauma hypotheses. Although we have

(1915-1963); (a) castration anxiety, (b) separation anxiety, (c) the primal scene, and the (d) Oedipus complex (that includes birth, the loss of the mother as an exclusive love and sexual object, penis envy, the possible loss of the object's love, and the loss of the super-ego's love) (Khan, 1963).

moved further within Freudian discourse, his clinical and theoretical notations did bring into sharp focus not only the impact of the Other on the inner life of the child, but that which is created endopsychically also holds the ability to overwhelm the child throughout his or her development. Concerning this protective function as well as its 'failures', countless theorists have accentuated that without such functioning, that is, the parent as *psychological guardian, protector, elucidator, enhancer, clarifier and scaffolder, the psyche remains vulnerable to flooding*. Khan further states that the phenomena of cumulative trauma reflects the continuous "breaches in the mother's role as a protective shield over the whole course of the child's development" and that the "breaches in the mother's role as protective shield are qualitatively and quantitatively different from those gross intrusions by the mother's acute psychopathology...In this context it would be more accurate to say that these breaches over the course of time and through the developmental process *cumulate silently and invisibly*. Hence the difficulty in detecting them clinically in childhood. They gradually get embedded in the specific traits of a given character structure. *Also, they achieve the value of trauma only cumulatively and in retrospect*" (Khan, 1963, pp. 290-291).

Supported by further relational insights, analysts such as Bernard Brandchaft (2010), Margaret Crastnopol (2015) and existential phenomenologists such as Todd DuBose (2014), all faithfully describe how the self adapts to shock and strains traumas. Crastnopol's (2015) psychoanalytic vision especially focusses on micro-trauma and she articulates the following constellations:

- Unkind cutting back
- Connoisseurship gone awry
- Uneasy intimacy
- Psychic airbrushing and excessive niceness
- Chronic entrenchment and its collateral damage
- Unbridled indignation

- Little murders and other everyday micro-assaults

It will be the aim of the current paper to address and make use of selected micro-traumas as defined by Dr Crastnopol. The reader is, however, advised to read Dr Crastnopol's work in detail. It is a transforming psychoanalytic treasure. I will also add another micro-trauma easily overlooked in western society, 'Killing with Kindness', as well as include separately, although part of Dr Crastnopol's book, the concept of pathological accommodation by the late Dr Bernard Brandchaft (2010). I now turn to the various micro traumas in service of Dasein-icide.

Little Murders, Everyday Micro-assaults and Non Recognition of Other

Little murders and other micro- assaults on Being include; "A vast and various group of behaviors, they include off-hand insults, slights, mockery, back-biting, discounting, damning with faint praise, and back-handed compliments" (Crastnopol, 2015, p.187). Any critique that focuses on one's *intrinsic value* as a human being, being treated with contempt, being ignored or minimized, as well as the subjective experience of being continuously countered, if not flooded, by a mono-culture (I am right-you are wrong) could function as an everyday micro assault[9]. Micro–assaults frequently create an attitude of silence and withdrawal, as a way to safeguard the autochthonous self. Analysands frequently allow for the emergence of painful themes of such assaults and the non-recognition of Being it engenders (even in the analytic dyad[10]). Kohutian and intersubjectivists all articulate this domain with much sensitivity and have created language to enhance appreciation of the complex interplay between our need for self-esteem nutriment and refueling, and the variations the Other can serve in strengthening our inner sense of value and goodness (mirroring, idealizing, twinship transferences). Examples may suffice. In a more classical example a young emotionally intense analysand caught in a *Tantalus complex* reflected; "I wish I had a

9 Also see the work of Derald Wing Sue entitled *Micro-aggressions in everyday life* (2010, pp. 31-34) for his own taxonomy.
10 The work of Lakoff, R.B. & Coyne, J.C. (1993) entitled *Father knows best: the use and abuse of power in Freud's case of Dora* comes to mind.

penis—I always felt left out by my father...my father and brother would go fishing but I could not go cause I could not wee off the side of the boat...I was left out cause I was a girl. That is why I do sports that I can compete with men - show them I can do it. I would also clean my father's car, even with earbuds! Wanted it perfect for him. He said: 'great, very well done, but remember there is always room for improvement!'" Again one can read, as it became evident throughout the therapy, that the analysand found herself always out of reach of the father's ideal and true tender presence—a desirable deserter. From a literary position the work of Franz Kafka[11] "A letter to my father" remains a literary treasure reflecting very similar moments of non-recognition of self.

Affective Overdrive, Engulfment and Gushing

The latter can be defined as the emotional and psychological flooding of another (with both positive or negative affect), foreclosing reciprocity and dialogical space; "the ardent person in overdrive expresses him or herself quite forcefully, with a long and strong flow of feeling" (Crastnopol, 2015, p.195). In affective overdrive the recipient may feel drowned or taken over by the other to such an extent that "the recipient may lose touch with his her inner psychological experience"(Crastnopol, 2015, p.195). Again the variations and permutations here are legion, and it should be added that the engulfer, gusher, or one in overdrive may do so paradoxically to protect themselves from feeling flooded, controlled or abandoned (affect as glue). Tragic consequences ensue. An astute and sensitive analysand reported the following:

> "Spent time with mother again...she truly becomes different in her absence... *with her I am shocked again*.... Eigen talks about the importance of having an experience that is nerve to nerve... for me it's a painful immediate experience. I have this area on my back, eczema.... she sees the spot and tells me she has a cream that could help. I said thank you and I would put it on—she said she wanted to... she went on and on and on. She was so upset! She actually started crying that I would not allow

11 A special thank you to Ms. Annelies Cramer for introducing this work to me. Deeply therapeutic.

> her to do it—that I would not allow her to take care of me. Seriously! So I allow her—I gave in. As she put it on she keeps on rubbing it in, rubbing it in, rubbing it in. I didn't like that. She reacts as if I withheld something from her..... it's all about her need, not my comfort. I feel manipulated. It is like exaggerated affect! It's a small thing in ordinary situations...She told me that she is very grateful to have me...She told me that she would walk and sooth me as an infant for hours by crying and telling me all her 'grief'—*she lavished bad times on me*... This is disturbing for me—as an adult at least I can show some resistance, I can say to her—I don't want to hear it!"

The analysand goes on to describe many instances of having to protect herself, from childhood onward, from mother's unreflexively sharing of private content; "As if she did not save me from her private content—she did not protect me!"

Sin Eaters—Matyrdom, Emotional Blackmail and Coercion

It has been evident in countless psychoanalytic works that many struggle to differentiate from their primary relationships, and when they do, they experience immense survivor guilt as they have been subjected to martyrdom parenting/relating; "oh, don't trouble yourself—I will sit here in the dark". Seemingly altruistic and non-demanding, martyrdom hides the deep impact of intrapsychic and interpersonal extortion as it co-opts another's psychic state, capacities and the fundamental human need for intrapsychic freedom, generating anxiety, guilt, and shame if one does activate, or enjoys separateness. This has been artfully described in Sartre's Flaubert studies (House of Nauseating Recurrence, 1981) and the work of Rudyard Kipling (House of Desolation, in Shengold, 1999). I remain astounded by their brilliance and sensitivity. One possible adaptation to this micro-trauma is found in what I referred to as sin eaters, i.e., those that carry the burden of depressive masochistic struggles, forever caught within the field of a *seraph introject*. An analysand (Jill) with burning mouth syndrome described her relationship with her mother as "100%", that she was "*really one with her (mother)*". Paradoxically, it was also this perfect mother that Jill experienced as a strict disciplinarian, restricting her daily activities with punishment (physical).

Jill was constantly watched over; rarely allowed to venture outside the house, and had no friends or supporting family. Although the closeness was initially experienced as "good", i.e., her school years, adult life proved problematic—excessive compliance, returning home to be with mum, and stifling the need to explore and expand her psychic horizons became areas of conflict. Jill did move 'against' the status but was usually met with grave consequences; "I got cheeky, when I was not allowed to do what I wanted. Mother used to slap me in the face when I did get cheeky". The latter also served as basis for various psychosomatic symptoms (bruxism, later burning mouth syndrome) and persecutory dreams. The closeness foreclosed many adult avenues at autonomous self-expression, individuation and self-support, and after Jill's mother passed away, Jill was left emotionally destitute, isolated, and deprived of a full and creative life.

Killing with Kindness

It may seem paradoxical that kindness can be experienced as burdensome in relationships. Julie, a deeply private, if not schizoid analysand communicated this reality as follows: "It is difficult to describe, but being in hospital is extremely stressful, not just the fact that I am under the influence of other's care, their way of doing, but they actually act and think that their help is *only but good*. If you say 'no' it immediately changes their approach to you. At times they think—'oh, she is old'. They can decide. What frightens me is that they can even send people to your house to be 'helpful'." It can certainly be said that such analysands are just sensitive, as I have frequently heard, although it avoids the deep reality that dependency, at times, comes with a kindness that has its own order and ministration, if not technocracy. The analysand made me aware of a multitude of 'attitudes', some seemingly benign ('Oh—it's 'cause she has grey hair'), and its impact in how relationships are morally 'intended' and 'structured' ala Harry Stack Sullivan. Although couched in 'I am doing this 'cause' I want to do good' the aphorism 'The road to hell is paved with good intentions/ Hell is full of good meanings, but heaven is full of good works', comes to mind. In two creative works (Jones, 2009; Pond & Palmer, 2016), written by mental health specialists, killing with kindness as dasein-icide is thoughtfully addressed, that is, mental health practices that make use of compliance and surrender (AA for example) as an overarching strategy run various unrecognized psychological risks. They argue that relational contexts designed in authoritarian fashion (although seen as caring) could re-evoke pathological accommodative transference-counter-transference matrixes, unwittingly eclipsing the undernourished selves of the very persons they are trying to support, repeating a variation of dasein-icide.

Wearing Teflon, Spoiling, Deception and Pathological Accommodation

According to Crastnopol (2015); "Wearing Teflon is the ability to slough off one's flaws or mistakes, and is often accompanied by the tendency to externalize and attribute them to someone or something else" (p. 204). Crastnopol's description seems very reminiscent of Neo-Kleinian Gianna Williams's (1998) concept of the 'no-entry' system of defense. The 'no-entry' system of defense is part of the *Omega function,* wherein the Other is not only impervious to frustration, but is also overflowing with projections. The *Omega function* may be viewed as part of the disorganized-disorientated attachment style, where patients have been exposed to frightening and frightened parents, usually both. As obdurate/obstructive Other (Eaton, 2005), in contrast to serving as a welcoming Other, the recipient of such relational interaction (again over time) may adopt accommodative attitudes, rebel, or collapse a viable sense of self. It is especially virulent where the Other feels always in the right ('Mother knows best'), spoils attempts at differentiation and individuation, and approaches the other from within a paradigm of paternalistic deception. 'For your own good' is thus used to justify running interference with a *person's liberty and sense of freedom.* The work of Alice Miller (1981, 1988, 1994) remains a testament to such cultural and interpersonal practices. It is not difficult to envision that there are relational dyads and cultural trends that function under the shadow of the *Omega function* and thus serve as psychological soil to a 'fitting in' (giving in) agenda, a false *Dasein* that forecloses a creative mandate to live from the True Self. In its extreme, it could foreshadow the death of desire (Thompson, 2017), a divided self pervaded by ontological insecurity (Laing, 1960). Central to Dr Brandchaft's clinical sensibilities he defines "pathological accommodation" at the root of such states of mind:

> "The term *accommodation* refers to the child's response to this relational trauma, for children adjust to threats to their attachment relationships by attempting *to fit in with* their caretaker's world when their caretaker cannot recognize and respond to theirs. The needs and feelings of the parent are then privileged by the child at the expense of the child's authentic self experience." (2010, p. 3)

Similar to the beautiful poem by Shel Silverstein entitled *Obedient* (in *Falling Up*, p. 90) an analysand I will refer to as Ruth, consulted me after her physician was concerned about her depression. I was able to learn from Ruth the power of possessive love and *being strangled into life*. According to Ruth:

> "Mother is always right" and "you are always wrong", "would tell me what to do, think and even what to dress. I was not allowed to do things by myself, like visit friends, she followed me everywhere. I even slept with her until I was 23. I took it till I was early 30s, I started saying no, going out. She would react with stress, at times crying throughout the night and say; 'how could you do this to me, after all I have done'. One day she went for my throat, tried to strangle me... My mother buried me in her horrible youth. I felt so responsible for her—that was my jail... I had a dark night of the soul."

Connoisseurship Gone Awry

Connoisseurship gone awry can be defined as a style of relating where one partner in the dyad acts like a hyper discriminating "master". The master exposes the other to a process of exact thinking and reasoning, or an *excessively reasoned train of thought* (being ratiocinative). Caught within a hermeneutic of suspicion the recipient is always found to be 'not-quite-there-yet', always to be bettered, caught in the so called Pygmalion Effect as described by Robert Rosenthal. The recipient is continuously undercut, their sense of agency and esteem minimized. An analysand I will call Margaret described this reality (scoliotic transference in our work) as follows; "My mother could not leave a room without saying what is wrong with it...adjust things continuously...Since she had scoliosis all was a constant adaptation for her. She was crooked... You would never say or know it, as she adjusted all her clothes....She was like that with us - it was actually a sign of love if she would say to you - that scarf makes you look unattractive. You look attractive ... if only your chin wasn't so. ...Mum would include and be positive towards all other people, but with me and my siblings she was different. We had to do everything perfectly - we all had to be a certain way....mum had scoliosis and she was diagnosed with an axis 1 too..."

I recall a particularly important experience with Margaret that served as a window into her micro-trauma. We were experiencing a period of intense rainfall, so much so that I used a small towel in front of the waiting room door for clients to dry their shoes. As Margaret entered the waiting room I was met with a scathing remark about its inappropriateness and I was left, not so much in the moment, but actually in her later absence, with a feeling of shame, embarrassment and a need to ensure it never to happen again. It became *suddenly an eye sore*. It was thus of psychological interest to later learn that Margaret developed cataracts after a severe separation experience. Both Rudyard Kipling and the psychoanalyst Harry Guntrip write about living in strict, unforgiving and exacting households, and all of these writers, as well as my analysand developed visual symptoms after traumas of separation. The price of being an eye sore?

Soul Blindness and Optic Rectomitis

Soul blindness can be characterized as the inability to see that a child, or the Other for that matter, possesses a unique sense of self, mind, interiority, or Soul. The dasein-psychoanalyst Eric Craig (2008) gives a touching account what could be meant by using the concept Soul, i.e., *as one's gathering of lived experience as unique to that situated life lived*; "In saying that the gathering of life-lived experience is situated, I mean only that as *Da-sein*, our gathering of experience is unavoidably contextualized, that is, shaped and structured by the manifold social, historical, existential, genetic, biological, and evolutionary contexts from which each of our existences arise." (p. 259). As such the Soul remains forever unique, sacred, a true archive of a life lived. It should be approached with the same respect as a revered text. An analysand, Timothy explained the impact of its absence as follows; "My father, he had *optic rectomitis.* Nothing I did or said what good—all shit! He didn't teach me anything but criticized all I did. He was never wrong, would never apologize and would say the most ridiculous things, like you cannot trust a man that has a beard—things like that, blatantly wrong!" Another analysand, with similar father experiences used the term "*negatosis*" to describe the intrapsychic 'talking' residue of parental demand that would continuously run commentary on his performance, his sense of self, never allowing him a moment of psychic rest. Another analysand, Lea, believed that due to her mother's inability to truly see her, she never understood "the secret world of adults" and believed, similar to the song of *Pat Benatar* that "Hell is for children"; "I had to be like a trained seal, had to give a show...: I am pondering it, when did it start.... as a kid....*little things*...I removed myself from my body.....body is a vessel only, put my mind somewhere else, preservation, protect myself...."

Psychic Airbrushin and Excessive Niceness

In this reality mother and infant are disclosed to each other in various ways; the mother 'touches', in the Heideggerian sense, her infant and child with a specific mood, vision and state of mind. She loves, she envisions, and dreams her child through her ministrations, and as such the child will be informed of its existence within the maternal orbit. Concrete biological existence is given psychic meaning—it is this contact with the world by being 'touched' that the maternal imprint, the unconscious mothering of the primordial Other is set in motion. The infant, like the mother, and the mother before her all struggle with the tension between the autochthonous drive and encountering the alienating experiences contact brings, as well as fated situations. It is so that the dyad can be infused by what I see as *techniques of goodness*, as I refer to them. In Crastnopol's (2015) taxonomy it can be referred to as psychic airbrushing and excessive niceness. This is certainly not the same as idealization, more so:

> "In airbrushing, the minimization of flaws is on a different level than it would be in idealization; it is more day to day,

> regular operating procedure than a psychic cleavage. And it subtly makes the disavowed faults that much harder to register and react to or compensate for. Also, in addition to the component of denial, certain "beautification" process occurs in airbrushing that more fully contradicts the possibility of there being any badness to begin with. Being subtle and therefore stealthful in its destructiveness is a feature common to all micro-trauma mechanisms" (p. 116).

It is as if disillusioned parts of the self and the other is sequestered off, overtly or covertly; "Of course you are very good at that, all my kids are, you are just imagining that that is not so!" Parental airbrushing can be devastating to a child's growing ability to know the mind of the Other, the 'truth' of a situation, and to be able to perceive reality and its vicissitudes. It is also true that if the parent continuously 'airbrushes' the child—the child may never know reality as is, and as such the reality of limitations.

Airbrushing can also be combined with denial and other defense mechanism coloring perception and self experience. After ensuring time with his parents (both were remarried), an analysand mentions that two separate experiences left him bereft of parental involvement and support. Each time he was to meet a parent they cancelled and provided excuses that seemed illogical. Worse, it made him feel as if he was impinging on/ in their worlds. Paradoxically both parents would later text and say that they had a 'great time', that they hoped he had too, making the analysand feel guilty about his needs and feelings as well. Any attempt to address emotional difficulty in the family was met with 'make nice' and further silencing strategies.

Soul Murder

In two poignant psychoanalytic works (Williams, 2010, 2013), neither a case study *per se*[12] nor an autobiography, the psychoanalyst Paul Williams (2010) describes various ways a mind/soul survives a developmental *wakemare*, i.e, being an "one unknown, unchronicled creature" (2010, p.103):

12 "The author of this book, and the individual written about, are not the same person. It is a piece of literature that furnishes an account of the methods of a mind in its efforts to prevail in oppressive circumstances" (Williams, 2010 from the *Preface*)

> "The scale of deprivation was not due primarily to economic poverty... My parents hated other people, so that living together, being a family was torture. The lack of stimulation in childhood was punctuated by outbursts of capricious violence that were a feature of my mother's psychotic personality and my parent's disastrous relationship. Emptiness and numbness were the backcloth to my and my sister's experience of violence...We were conditioned, in our retreat into silence, to expect attack whenever we were in the house. As a result, I found myself living in two contradictory states of mind. One was a persistent need to get food, whilst avoiding being savaged, and the other was an unrequited craving to find respite from these threats of violence and pressure to survive..." (pp. 116-117).

Severe deprivation (understimulation) as well as overstimulation, if not a combination of the two, sees the creation of a lived world characterized by a sense of pressure, cravings, being short circuited, frightened, split (gut-mind), push-pulled, unable to relax, and having no respite. The psychoanalyst Shengold (2011) adds, in his description of Soul Murder,

> "Soul murder is a crime in which the perpetrator is able to destroy the victim's capacity for feeling joy and love." (p.121).

Whereas Sartre's work describes predominantly what I would consider soul blindness, it is evident that in soul murder the neglect and abuse experienced is to such an extent that a feral existence seems preferable, although it could be hidden to general observation. Jane, a chronically emotionally starved analysand, stated it as follows: "I get along with people, I have learned to 'track' in relationships. But if I am cornered, made to be and feel frightened, I turn feral, a street-kid, dangerous. I do not trust people". The writings of child psychiatrist Bruce Perry (Perry & Szalavitz, 2006) gives testament to many such adaptations, especially his work entitled "The boy who was raised as a dog". The examples given by Williams are vivid and extreme in the sense that the 'hero' in the narratives (2010, 2013) suffered from clear cut abuse and neglect. Shengold's work also gives examples, but of a more insidious variation, of soul murder, some I have come to see in especially narcissistic family and religious-cultural practices, wherein the presence of *childism*, to use Young – Bruehl's term (2012), seems ever present. Within such families and environmental *practices*, the following may be encountered: milieu control, demand for unquestioned loyalty (allegiance), authoritarianism, intimidation, myths of infallibility, the punishing of any deviation, scapegoating, shaming, holding doctrine over person (i.e. ideology/propaganda programming), a demand for purity, and forced confession ('tell the truth you little liar'). Many describe soul murder as being endopsychically *gutted*, being nullified, guillotined, eclipsed, entombed, marooned, exiled, being unchronicled, and falling into oblivion; "What happened to me... I lost belief, any trust in my gut, damaged trust instincts.... I have a mind-gut split... my love instinct has been damaged... to feel is to fear."

Conclusion

Obstructive and micro-trauma processes, from childhood onward, run the risk of swallowing, enslaving, colonizing, and entrapping the native self in various accommodative strategies. Freedom from entrenchment and being overwhelmed, poses unique challenges to the native self, seeing a lifelong pattern of deep psychological, if not soulful, struggle. This paper, similar to the work of Khan, Laing, Eigen, Crastnopol, Brandchaft and Shengold, set forth the languaging of such soul deprivation and tragedy, with the hope that openings may exist, and freedom found.

Bibliography

Bakan, D. (1971). *Slaughter of the innocents.* San Francisco: Jossey-Bass, Inc.

Bion, W. R. (1957). Differentiation of the psychotic from the non-psychotic personalities. *International Journal of Psychoanalysis,* 38, 266–75.

Bion, W. R. (1958). On hallucination. *International Journal of Psychoanalysis,* 39, 341–9.

Bion, W. R. (1959). Attacks on linking. *International Journal of Psychoanalysis,* 40, 308–15.

Brandchaft, B., Doctors, S., & Sorter. D. (2010). *Towards an emancipatory Psychoanalysis. Brandchaft's intersubjective vision.* New York and London: Routledge, Taylor & Francis Group.

Craig, E. (2008). The Human and the hidden: existential wondering about depth, soul, and the unconscious. *Humanistic psychologist,* 36, 227-282.

Crastnopol, M. (2015). *Micro-trauma. A psychoanalytic understanding of cumulative psychic injury.* New York and London: Routledge, Taylor & Francis Group.

DuBose, T. (2014). Personal communication.

Eaton, J. E. (2005). The obstructive object. *Psychoanalytic Review,* 92 (3), 355–72.

Eigen, M. (1977). On working with "unwanted" patients. *International Journal of Psychoanalysis,* 58, 109–21.

Eigen, M. (1981). The area of faith in Winnicott, Lacan and Bion. *International Journal of Psychoanalysis,* 62, 413–33.

Eigen, M. (1983). Dual union or undifferentiation? A critique of Marion Milner's view of the sense of psychic creativeness. *International Review of Psycho-Analysis*, 10, 415–28.

Eigen, M. (1985). Toward Bion's starting point: Between catastrophe and faith. *International Journal of Psychoanalysis*, 66, 321–30.

Eigen, M. (1986). *The Psychotic Core*. London: Karnac (2004)

Eigen, M. & Phillips, A. (Ed.). (1993). *The Electrified Tightrope*. London: Karnac (2004).

Eigen, M. (1995). Psychic deadness: Freud. *Contemporary Psychoana*lysis, 31 (2), 277–99.

Eigen, M. (1996). Psychic deadness. London: Karnac (2004).

Eigen, M. (1999). *Toxic Nourishment*. London: Karnac.

Eigen, M. (2001). *Damaged Bonds*. London: Karnac.

Eigen, M. (2004). *The Sensitive Self*. Middletown, CT: Wesleyan University Press.

Eigen, M. (2007). *Feeling Matters*. London: Karnac.

Freud, S. (1915). Instincts and Their Vicissitudes. *Standard Edition XIV*. London: Hogarth, 1957.

Freud, S. (1920). Beyond the Pleasure Principle. *Standard Edition XVIII*. London: Hogarth Press, 1950.

Freud, S. (1923). The Ego and the Id. *Standard Edition XIX*. London: Hogarth Press, 1961 .

Freud, S. (1926). Inhibitions, Symptoms and Anxiety. *Standard Edition XX*. London: Hogarth Press, 1959.

Grotstein, J. S. (1997). Integrating One-Person And Two-Person Psychologies: Autochthony And Alterity In

Counterpoint. *Psychoanalytic Quarterly*, 66, 403-430.

Janoff-Bulmn, R. (1992). *Shattered assumptions—towards a new psychology of trauma*. New York: The Free Press.

Jones, D.B. (2009). Addiction and pathological accommodation: an intersubjective look at impediments to the utilization of alcoholics anonymous. *International Journal of Psychoanalytic Self Psychology*, 4, 212-234.

Kafka, F. (2017). *Letter to my fat*her. Alma Classics.

Khan, M. R. (1960). Regression and integration in the analytic setting: A clinical essay on the transference and counter-transference aspects of these phenomena. *International Journal of Psychoanalysis*, 41, 130–46.

Khan, M. R. (1963). The concept of cumulative trauma. *Psychoanalytic Study of the Child*,18, 286–306.

Khan, M. R. (1971). Infantile neurosis as a false-self organization. *Psychoanalytic Quarterly*, 40, 245–63.

Khan, M. R. (1972). Dread of surrender to resourceless dependence in the analytic situation. *International Journal of Psychoanalysis*, 53, 225–30.

Lakoff, R.T. & Coyne, J.C. (1993). *Father knows best. The use and abuse of power in Freud's case of Dora*. New York: Teachers College, Columbia.

Lang, R.D. (1960). *The divided self.* London: Tavistock.

Miller, A. (1981). *Thou shalt not be aware. Society's betrayal of the child*. New York: A meridian book.

Miller, A. (1988). *Banished knowledge. Facing childhood injuries.* New York: Doubleday.

Miller, A. (1994). *For your own good. Hidden cruelty in child rearing and the roots of violence*. New York: Noonday

Press.

Perry, B.D, & Szalavitz, M. (2006). *The boy who was raised as a dog and other stories from a child psychiatrist's notebook.* NY: Basic Books.

Pond, M. & Palmer, M. (2016). *Wasted. An alcoholic therapist's fight for recovery in a flawed treatment system.* Canada: Greystone Books, Ltd.

Sartre, J.P. (1981). *The family idiot: Gustave Flaubert, 1821-1857, Volume 1.* Chicago: University of Chicago Press.

Shengold, L. (1999). *Soul murder. Thoughts about therapy, hate, love and memory.* New Haven and London: Yale University Press.

Shengold, L. (2011). Trauma, soul murder, and change. *Psychoanalytic Quarterly, LXXX,* 1, 121-138.

Silverstein, S. (2006). *Falling up.* NY: Harper Collins

Sue, D.W. (2010). *Microaggression in everyday life. Race, gender, and sexual orientation.* New Jersey: John Wiley and Sons.

Thompson, M.G. (2017). *The death of desire. An existential study in sanity and madness.* London and New York: Routledge, Taylor and Francis Group.

Vonnegut, K. (2010). *Welcome to the monkey house.* New York: Random House, Inc.

Willliams, G. (1998). *Internal Landscapes and Foreign Bodies: Eating disorders and other pathologies.* London: Routledge (Tavistock Clinic Series).

Winnicott, D. W. (1945). Primitive emotional development. *International Journal of Psychoanalysis,* 26, 137–43.

Winnicott, D. W. (1958). The capacity to be alone. *International*

Journal of Psychoanalysis, 39, 416–20.

Winnicott, D. W. (1960). The theory of the parent–infant relationship. *International Journal of Psychoanalysis*, 41, 585–95.

Winnicott, D. W. (1969). The use of an object. *International Journal of Psychoanalysis*, 50, 711-6.

Winnicott, D. W. (1974). Fear of breakdown. *International Review of Psycho-Analysis*, 1, 103–7.

Willliams, G. (1998). *Internal Landscapes and Foreign Bodies: Eating disorders and other pathologies.* London: Routledge (Tavistock Clinic Series).

Williams, P. (2010). *The fifth element.* London: Karnac Books.

Williams, P. (2013). *Scum.* London: Karnac Books.

Young-Bruehl, E. (2012). *Childism. Confronting prejudice against children.* London: Yale University Press.

Primacy of the Individual as the Bearer of Moral Law: The Psychoanalysis of Otto Rank and Kantian Ethics

Julio Roberto Costa, MS

Summary

Otto Rank posed the human question of the search for permanence by means of the symbolic life, which includes belonging to a group that the individual identifies himself or herself with. Historically, this has been seen in the tribe, the clan, the nation, etc., as a unit that needs to be asserted in opposition to other groups. Ernest Becker emphasized that this affirmation of the symbolic value of the belonging to a group needed the denial of the value of others. In fact, Otto Rank saw in it the real source of conflict and warfare[1].

However, insofar as Rank can be considered an exponent of German idealism, we must assume a space of freedom of the individual, which can be conceived of as grounded in Kantian moral philosophy. Thus, if what characterizes the human subject are the choices freely made by reason, we find that the human being in Rank's works has a freedom of choice, a thought we can identify as the product of Kantian influence. Therefore, I intend to present Rank's texts as consistent with Immanuel Kant's legacy, mainly regarding practical reason. We can assume that, through these choices in relation to moral acting, the affirmation of the being of the individual does not necessarily require the overcoming of the other—that is, dispensing of violence—although it indeed sheds new light on the violence within society.

Considering Ernest Becker's views of violence and society in conjunction with Otto Rank's emphasis on the individual as the bearer of moral law, a Kantian influence, there is solid ground for the observation that social ordering is a human construction.

Rather than a neutral entity, social ordering generates nuclei of

1 Otto Rank, *Beyond Psychology* (New York: Dover Publications Inc, 1958), 40.

power to empower some at the expense of the majority. From this study, we must conclude that, to foster ethics, these social relationships need to become more akin to the moral law that lies in the individual.

Introduction

The work of Otto Rank brings many challenges for those who study it. Although highly rich in the meaning and depth of analysis, Rank's concepts are diffuse throughout his work. Moreover, after Rank was excluded from the Vienna Psychoanalytic Society, it seems he knew he would not be understood, and, as E. James Lieberman stated in his biography of Rank, *Acts of Will*, he was considered a pariah[2].

This may pertain to the fact that he had no way of forming a school or having his own students.

Of utmost importance in his books is the inclusion of philosophy, especially that of the great ethicist Immanuel Kant; of Arthur Schopenhauer, who demonstrated the world as an expression of the will; and the young Friedrich Nietzsche, the great pragmatist who saw that the necessity of the affirmation of being—itself based on the will, the only existing subject—had primacy over the conceptual or moral judgement of that expression.

The question of death and finitude, as posed by Otto Rank, considers the search for a symbolic solution to the problem of the permanence of the individual, since in the world of nature this solution is impossible. Thus, according to Rank, all symbolic construction has, as its primary task, to place the human being above nature, which includes a connection with the symbolism of permanence of the groups in which the individual participates. This participation, such as in the clan, the tribe, or the nation, functions as a means of ensuring permanence by means of collective immortality, that is, through the group. This symbolic immortality needs to place the collectivity above nature and above other collectivities, and, drawing from

2 E. James Lieberman, *Acts of Will: The Life and Work of Otto Rank* (Amherst: University of Massachusetts Press, 1993), 286.

this thought, Ernest Becker emphasizes one aspect in Rank's work, namely, the challenge in achieving the symbolism of permanence of "our" group. Therefore, there is the propensity to justify the debunking, disqualifying, victimization, and even destruction of the other.

Foundations of Otto Rank's Psychoanalysis and the Question of Permanence

According to Otto Rank, the expression of the will in the human being, contrasting with his or her finitude and mortality, only finds a possible resolution through the symbolic repertoire of culture. The role of the individual in the legitimate development of himself or herself is to find expression in a creative way by contributing to the symbolic repertoire of the community.

The creative individual, the *artist,* produces meaning that validates his or her own expression in the world. The individual does so against the pressure for conformity, and has an inner experience of the dynamic of will, guilt, and affirmation, to achieve his or her goal. However, the individual will not disassociate himself or herself from the community. Although Rank's emphasis is strongly on the individual, the individual's expression underlies an environment steeped in culture. We must assume, in that environment, the presence of a symbolic repertoire that is collective by its very nature. Therefore, this is an environment already akin to a collection of symbolic meanings, an environment that welcomes individual contributions to it. It is precisely this connection with the community that differentiates the creative and productive individual from the neurotic one, who lacks this connection[3]. The neurotic, instead of creatively and positively affirming his or her will and value, will feel the difference sorrowfully, perceiving it to be a reflection of his or her inferiority and displacement from the collective.

Likewise, Rank asserts that artistic expression is collective in its origin. In primitive societies, the work of art was social rather than individual, reflecting the communal partaking of the pleasurable experience of the affirmation of the human

3 Otto Rank, *Truth and Reality*, trans. Jessie Taft (New York: W.W. Norton & Company Inc., 1978), 173.

will inside the world[4]. Thus, the individual offers content to the community, re-signifying and re-elaborating the pre-existing symbology, to bring legitimate and sincere meaning to his or her place in the world. The individual becomes, increasingly, a subject that brings meaning to life, in a social world that is fulfilled by shared meaning. Symbology is, thus, a means of social integration for the individual. But let us observe the directions that the personal will can take. Kantian thought would lead us to conclude that the individual needs to seek autonomy, which entails affirming the right to make his or her own choices. Heteronomy is the negation of the subject, and autonomy is his or her affirmation. It becomes necessary, therefore, to deny everything that can debunk the person. Often, the tendency is to think of this as submission as imposed from the outside world, although, with the influence of Immanuel Kant, Rank asserts that biological determinisms, insofar as they are like the concept of *inclinations* in Kantian moral philosophy, are also perceived by the subject as a coercion against individual will. At this point we can introduce some of Ernest Becker's positions. In Becker's view, this affirmation of the symbolic aspect can be viewed as the construction of an *alter-organism*[5], which means a symbolic nature that overlaps with the biological organism, to remove from consciousness the remembrance of the biological limits to existence. As we have already seen, so far as biological perpetuation is impossible, it will be necessary to search for symbolic perpetuation—the denial of death.

An important unfolding of the denial of death will be the mechanisms of social division between "we" and "they," which will have the function of separating those who are supposed to deserve immortality ("we") from those who are supposed to be the outcasts of the world and who deserve to be discharged—in other words, "they." Becker grounds himself on Otto Rank when he tells us that the desire for permanence in the human being seeks a symbology of collective immortality so that personal immortality can be assured through the permanence of the clan, the tribe, the nation, or the like.

4 Otto Rank, *Art and Artist*, trans. Charles Francis Atkinson (New York: W.W. Norton & Company Inc., 1989), 397.

5 Ernest Becker, *La Lucha Contra el Mal*, trans. Carlos Valdés (México: Fondo de Cultura Económica, 1992), 20.

From the point of view of the need for symbolic permanence, this is the origin of the victimization of all the human collectives that are considered different, as well as the real origin of warfare. According to Rank, when a group feels the need to consider itself a special one, above all the others, that has the fate to offer symbolic permanence exclusively to its peers, then it becomes permissible, indeed consistent, to "exclude the different ones from the blessings of eternity"[6].

Otto Rank's Psychoanalysis and the Legacy of Kant

The will, as understood by Schopenhauer and Nietzsche, was not the only important consideration for Otto Rank. Also, important to him were *acts* of will, capable of being made by an autonomous subject who has choices. Autonomy is the ability of reason to make choices, the moment it confronts itself and needs to get answers to the question: "how should I act?". In the criticism exercised at this point, that is, within the boundaries of what can be known or thought by the human being, Kant made morality a practical subject of reason, placing a boundary on the seduction of useless metaphysical speculation.

In Kantian philosophy, the distinction between what can be known and what can only be thought of is basic. All things that can be known can be thought of, but there are things that can be thought of but cannot be known. Knowledge comes from the sensible world, and thus we cannot know that which does not give us any sensory impression. In this way, Kant tells us that speculative reason, when it seeks to know what does not generate sensible experience, finds nothing, and from there everything that is said will be metaphysical—that is, in Kant's words, deception and illusion from speculative reason. Thus, it is important to note that what creates illusions is pure reason, insofar as it deals with an activity of which it has no sensible experience, which is, therefore, mere speculation. On the other hand, when reason has only itself and is confronted with the question "how should I act?", without being able to be guided by objects of sensible intuition, it will have to stand as the reason of a being who makes choices. At that point, it becomes practical reason, for actions will now be moved by choices, elected by means of freedom: "practical is all that is possible by

6 Rank, 1958, 41.

freedom".[7] At this point, the question would arise: but would this seemingly free choice not be moved by forces to which the subject himself has no access? What Kant places here is the problem of speculative reason in relation to things of which one has no sensible experience. When speculative reason tries to understand what does not generate sensible experience, the product of its activity can only be illusion. According to Kant, speculative reason created ancient metaphysics. Therefore, if there is a drive for practical choice, in the absence of any sensible experience, it is only possible, in terms of pure reason, to speculate about the nature of such a drive, which would lead to the creation of a new metaphysics of moral choice. In opposition to this, Kant emphasizes the fact that reason, when asked "how should I act?", must follow the way of the practical use:

> [Reason] Perceive objects that have a great interest for it. It enters the path of pure speculation to approach them, but they flee before it. Possibly, more success is to be expected in the only remaining path, that is, of practical use.[8]

Therefore, practical necessity overrides speculative theorizing, for, if we have no way of knowing, we are still forced to act, and we see the relevance of the question of practical action. Taking into consideration the absence of sensible experience when reason is faced with the choices of "how should I act?" this space of freedom needs to be postulated:

> . . . to know whether reason itself, in the acts by which it prescribes laws, is not determined in turn by other influences, and if what, in relation to the sensitive impulses, is called freedom, could not be, in relation to higher and distant causes, in turn, nature, in no way concerns us from the practical point of view, for we only ask reason, immediately, for the rule of conduct; it is, however, a simply speculative question, which we can put aside, since for our purpose we have only to do or fail to do. We thus know from experience practical freedom as a natural cause, namely as a causality of reason in the

7 Immanuel Kant, *Crítica da Razão Pura*, trans. Manuela Pinto dos Santos and Alexandre Fradique Morujão (Lisbon: Calouste Gulbenkian, 2001), 650.
8 Ibid., 645.

> determination of the will . . .[9].

Thus, in experience, the human being, while not having access to the noumenon as an object, is grounded on the intelligible world of the noumenon for his or her practical action. According to Kant, that which is practical is provided by freedom, which exists independently of the sensible and causal conditions of phenomena. Thus, even if the concept is, according to Kant, "theoretically empty," since it can have a moral utility, that is, a practical application, it cannot be neglected as a drive of human action and must therefore be thought of as real, despite of the fact that it cannot be known:

> [T]he concept of an entity that has free will is the concept of a *causa noumeno*. .
>
> .. Now the concept of an empirically unconditioned causality is, in fact, theoretically empty (without an intuition suited to it), yet always possible, and refers to an indeterminate object; although, on the other hand, it is given meaning in the moral law, therefore in a practical relation, so that in truth I do not possess any intuition that determines the theoretical objective reality, but it does not fail to have an effective application, which can present itself concretely in provisions or maxims, that is, to have practical reality that can be indicated.[10]

These practical choices will always reveal the major picture of the subject's belonging to a universe that has meaning by the action of the human being, and this meaning is actively shared by validating and revalidating the meaning that the individual partakes with the community, and, in turn, the meaning the community partakes with the individual. Thus, a meaning that is largely attributed by the individual is equally validated by the community, which requires from everyone a contribution to that creation of shared meaning.

Autonomy and Freedom

---

9 Ibid., 650.

10 André Gustavo Ferreira da Silva, Luís Lucas Dantas da Silva, "Kant: A Formação Moral como uma Tarefa Histórica da Espécie Humana, " *Espaço Pedagógico* vol. 21, no. 1 (Passo Fundo: Universidade de Passo Fundo, 2014), 133.

The central issue will be the treatment given to autonomy as an exercise of the will by the human being. According to the Kantian legacy, Rank gives a real role to autonomy, which must be well understood to situate the sense of Rank's theorizing within the history of thought. Here, it is relevant to remember that, in the preface to his book *Dawn*, Nietzsche, criticizing Kant, points out the fact that he has placed such morality in a place where it would be unscathed, dependent on a world that would be, by its turn, indemonstrable:

> . . . [Kant,] to give place to his "moral empire," found himself obliged to add an indescribable world, a logical "beyond" – that is why he needed his Critique of Pure Reason! In other words, he would not have needed her, had there not been one thing that mattered most to him – to make the "moral world" unassailable . .
>
> . . . [Kant] believed in morality, not because it was demonstrated by nature and history, but despite being incessantly contradicted by nature and history.[11]

However, this was a position that Kant clearly assumed, pertinent to the characteristics of the phenomenon and the noumenon, that is, while reason perceives in the sensible world *what happens* (phenomenon), in the intelligible world reason perceives what *should happen*, according to the practical laws of reason itself, and will therefore endeavor to succeed in the sensible world, as reason so establishes. Reason is, therefore, a *law-giving reason* and will become the practical use of that reason according to the laws of freedom, that is, autonomously, and not triggered by objects of the sensible world. Thus, Kant believes in morality not because it is demonstrated by nature and history, but precisely because it is not demonstrable by nature and by history, that is, by sensible experience. In this way, the will, consistent with the reason it needs to express itself as practice, needs to affirm the moral world within the world of phenomena. The will becomes *the practical use of reason*, that is, the affirmation of the autonomous choices of the human being, turning the empirical world, as much as possible, a space for the affirmation of these values:

11 Friedrich Nietzsche, *Aurora*, trans. Antônio Carlos Braga (São Paulo: Escala, 2007), 17–18.

> I call the moral world, the world insofar as it conforms to all moral laws (as it *can be*, according to the freedom of rational beings, and as it *should be*, according to the necessary laws of morality). The world is, thus, thought only as an intelligible world. . .. In this sense, then, it is a simple idea, albeit a practical one, that can and should really have its influence in the sensible world, to make it as much as possible according to this idea.[12]

Therefore, we must conclude that the moral world is realized not as a continuity of the external world of phenomena, but an affirmation of the inner will, that is, of the noumenon, in the face of the obstacles that the outside world offers to that expression. Thus, if the individual has the legitimacy to express an inner world that is not an extension of the world of phenomena, but rather is defined as an opposition to external coercion, he has a space of freedom that needs to be taken into consideration also in the question of symbolic permanence. One can see how much Rank's thinking becomes accessible by taking this Kantian context into account.

Permanence and Power in Ernest Becker

Ernest Becker is one of the great theorists about human destructiveness within the social sciences, focusing not on the instinctual aspect, concerning a medical and biological paradigm, but on the symbolic and cultural aspect. This question begins with the fact that the human being is conscious of his or her own finitude and thus has the consciousness of death. This awareness of finitude comes into conflict with the human capacity for symbolization in the question of creating the representation of his or her own ending. The individual sees himself or herself, at this moment, with the tension of being at once a biological being and a symbolic being. Discomfort arises with the condition of being a finite animal, which at the same time has a symbolic capacity, and thus can build a world of images that surpasses the earthly constraints.

In all situations in which an individual finds himself or herself confronted with this paradoxical reality, the individual perceives it as a contradiction and a threat, and tends to deny

12 Kant, 2001, 653.

his or her finite condition, necessitating, for that goal, to deny the biological reality—hence, the denial of death. Adding to this, the question is not only dying, but to die and remain forgotten, that is, to be insignificant in history, having no importance for a world that can exist without him. As Becker writes, "to have importance is to be enduring, to have life"[13]. Thus, following the thought of Otto Rank, Becker asserts that symbolic systems exist to raise the human being above nature, so that the symbolic being realizes, at least in the consciousness of daily life, an overcoming of the biological being. To allow this, this overcoming allows necessary meanings of permanence on the fragile and fallible biological being. To this end, Becker tells us that culture coats the individual with an *alter-organism*—or, symbolic permanence.

Therefore, shared symbolic systems, which are legitimate in relation to an organism that has symbolic capacity, will also be committed to the task of denying finitude. But what could have been simply the sincere construction of the symbolic representations, pertinent to a being who possesses this faculty, will become a falsification of reality. It is necessary to emphasize that, being the other differentiated, his or her symbolic systems can be a challenge to the affirmation of the symbolic systems to which the individual attributes legitimacy. At this point, the other becomes a threat, for he can assert being in a different or opposite way, concerning another culture or another world view, and thus threatening the validity of the world view adopted by the individual.

It is possible to say that, in primitive societies, the feeling of permanence was achieved relatively harmlessly. Becker mentions John Huizinga and his book *Homo Ludens*[14], which stated that, for the primitive man, life was a joyful play, an everyday assertion of the value of everyone that protects the sense of value of each person together with the community, being "a rich and joyous dramatization of life".[15] Because there was nothing in these societies to compare with the legal, police, or military system of contemporary societies, it was sufficient

13 Becker, 1992, 35.
14 Johan Huizinga, *Homo Ludens*, trans. João Paulo Monteiro (São Paulo: Perspectiva, 2000), 53.
15 Becker, 1992, 38.

that a discouragement should be exercised, by means of the customs, in the sense that no one became too much above average, and consequently, a threatening overly powerful individual[16].

Becker associates the advent of the great social stratification with the increase of the cultural emphasis in the individual. The reason is that, previously, the human being possessed the whole universe as a stage for the assertion of his or her value, but, progressively, he or she will only have the other person to validate or invalidate the construction of the individual self-esteem. We should note that, in nature, an individual always found affirmation, not because its elements (sun, moon, stars, forest, etc.) could not speak and contradict the individual, but because *everything in nature is an affirmation of being*. We can understand this by the thought of Schopenhauer, where the world is the *thing in itself*, the will, presenting itself in many disguised appearances.[17] By reading Rank, we can conclude that the true human values are the values of the affirmation of being. Thus, the man of ancient societies could easily feel "at home" in the world, but if, and only if, the symbolic capacity of his or her organism was properly backed up.

However, from the growing social division of labor, Becker argues that increasing asymmetry of power will accompany the scale of the construction of social inequality. Now, in a very asymmetric scenario, it becomes increasingly feasible to invalidate, discredit, disqualify, or even destroy, the other.

We can include, in this regard, the social construction of the *scapegoat* that must be sacrificed for the sake of community safety.[18] Ernest Becker continues this aspect of Rank's work by adding new contributions and building the path to what is now the *mortality salience* and the *terror management theory*[19]. One can thus verify the question of the exclusion of the other as a way of realizing a denial of mortality, as posited by Otto Rank

16 Becker, 1992, 145.

17 Arthur Schopenhauer, *O Mundo como Vontade e como Representação*, trans. Jair Barboza (São Paulo: UNESP, 2005), 160.

18 Becker, 1992, 180.

19 Sheldon Solomon, Jeff Greenberg and Tom Pysczcynski. "Tales from the Crypt: on the Role of Death in Life." *Zygon*, vol. 33, no. 1 (Chicago, Illinois: March 1988), 20.

and later developed by Ernest Becker.

In relation to the correct understanding of Otto Rank, the problem that Becker's understanding offers is the absence of a space of freedom. In Rank, this space of freedom exists as part of the influence of Immanuel Kant. As we have already stated, recognizing the Kantian heritage, and consequently German idealism, in Rank's thought can begin to clarify and deepen the understanding of many aspects of his work.

Violence from the Denial of Death and its Possible Overcoming

According to Hans Vaihinger, Nietzsche's radical doubts originated in the Kantian conception that one cannot know the thing in itself.[20] We can then conceive of the magnitude of this doubt, as Nietzsche tells us, and here we shall give the following example of this uncertainty about the reality of the world: suppose that there is in the world an object with a red color, although it appears to our eyes as being yellow, as the world possibly does not present itself to our senses as it really is. In turn, our senses are imperfect, and the eyes perceive the object as being green. The nervous stimulus, from the eyes to the brain, distorts the perception of the object, and our consciousness interprets it as being blue. So, with all this uncertainty about the world, let us now think of the relationship of two people, who we will call individual A and individual B. Both are willing to make their mutual relationship an ethical one. Individual A, at one point, says, "I have dignity; therefore, you should treat me with proper respect." Then, individual B could argue: "Wait, I'm going to get into the world of phenomena, to find evidence that what you said is true." However, in the world of phenomena one can only find that which generates a sensible experience, which is to say that nothing can be found about the moral world. With this emptiness, individual B can doubt individual A, and thus discredit him, disqualify him, and, consequently, oppress and, possibly, try to destroy him.

This consideration can give rise to several questions. In Rank, we see a compliance with the Kantian perspective, where we have the predominance of inner reason over coercion

20 Hans Vaihinger, *A Filosofia do Como Se*, trans. Johannes Kretschmer (Chapecó: Argos, 2011), 633.

exerted by the sensible world. In addition to such a conception, making full sense within the post-Kant German idealism, Rank himself classified his psychoanalysis in this way, by placing it as an affirmation of the will of the individual, despite external constraints against the expression of one's will.

At this point we must add the important question of society and the individual. The bearer of the will is the individual, or at most the community, but never the society. Society seeks to legitimize itself from the remains of the ideologies of immortality that have been useful to the individual and the community. When Rank writes about society, it is never in a way to legitimize it, in a movement of opposition to the individual, because the individual has the primacy, as bearer of the will and the moral law. It is possible here to feel the lack of a more precise conceptualization in Rank's thought, like that of the *primary groups* and *secondary groups*, such as exposed by Peter Berger and Thomas Luckmann[21], or of *sociality*, by Michel Maffesoli[22] , who contemplate groups more immediately familiar and friendly to the individual, in which there exist immediate relations and consensus, as opposed to the socioeconomic system. Those close groups are the ones the individual can rely on for support and protection, differing from the wider society. This larger society, in turn, becomes increasingly strange and threatening to the individual, and it thus takes on the contours of the concept of the socioeconomic system. Rank, for instance, makes it clear how much he considered that therapy could not, at the same time, stand on the side of the patient and the side of society. Society, posited as the formal and impersonal groups, constitutes a force of conformation of the person and the annulment of individuality.

The individual needs to express himself or herself with the help of the culture of his or her community, despite the normativity of the larger, impersonal society. Thus, we could say that the culture of the community, *as long as it is an expression of the will*, favors the expression of the individual will. On its turn,

---

21 Peter Berger, Thomas Luckmann, *A Construção Social da Realidade*, trans. Floriano de Souza Fernandes (Petrópolis: Vozes, 1985), 173.

22 Michel Maffesoli, *O Tempo das Tribos: o Declínio do Individualismo nas Sociedades de Massa*, trans. Maria de Lourdes Menezes (Rio de Janeiro: Forense Universitária, 1987), 9.

the great society, assuming a normative position, *as long as it is no more an expression of the will*, yearns to place limitations on the individual, which means it craves for social law in place of moral law. Social law, as Rank poses the concept, is the law instrumented by the groups in power for their own benefit, despite having its origin in moral law.

It becomes feasible to think that Rank recognizes society in the same way as Vaihinger's concept of an *intentionally created appearance* (bewusst gewollte Schein)[23], from the necessity of asserting an order even though it is known that this order is of a fictional nature. It may be concluded from Rank that he assumes that *society is not a bearer of the reason*. It is evident that Rank believes the will presents itself to the world not through society, but through the individual. Rank places the opposition of the individual and society in the following terms concerning therapy:

> For against this parent-like representative of the social will is aroused the self will of the weakest patient although it is interpreted by the Freudian therapist as resistance on the basis of his own will and in terms of his own moral and social ideals; that is, something that must be overcome or even broken instead of being furthered and developed. . .. Individual therapy degenerates into a mass education which is based on the traditional world view and the Jewish-Christian morality.[24]

We see that the individual—in this case, the patient—is in a position of social vulnerability, and moreover, in the face of a will fostered by the society that is historically situated within a specific cultural tradition (in this case, Jewish-Christian, although it could have been any other). Rank considered that the initial pessimism was repeated here in regard of the will, that is, the will is "bad," "inadequate," "immoral," and so on. In that historical context, to the extent that Freud advocated that men should live under a "dictatorship of reason," this would not be far from the truth.

The problem with this "dictatorship of reason," contrary to the

23 Vaihinger, 2011, 631. 24.
24 Rank, 1978, 22–23.

will, is that it would be heteronomous, coming from external constraints, which would have to control the instinctual life. However, Kantian morality requires the autonomy of the subject, precisely because this autonomy is the capacity of the will to determine itself by reason. That is, autonomy is an individual's autonomous choice to follow, in the moral world, duty, instead of his or her inclinations. However, the central point in proposing a "dictatorship of reason" is precisely to think of truth as an instance outside the individual. If this instance is society as it stands today, or as it will be in the future, it does not matter as much as a disqualification of the individual against outside powers that presumably have reason, and thus have the right to submit the individual. The valuation of the individual in Rank can be understood as the affirmation that the will is expressed, *par excellence*, through the individual, and not through society. Added to this, we can now conclude that, building on Schopenhauer, will is the force of nature in the individual, being the very manifestation of the being of the universe. In addition, Schopenhauer states that the will, in the human being, is the very foundation of ethics:

> From this point of view, it is undeniable that a system that places the reality of all existence and the root of the whole of nature in the will, detecting in this the heart of the universe, will have a great advantage in its favor. For it strikes, traversing a straight and simple path, and even has beforehand, before starting with ethics, what others seek to achieve only with long and always misleading deviations. In fact, this goal is truly unattainable, except through the notion that the force that drives action in nature, which presents this intuitive world to our intellect, is identical with the will in us. Only that metaphysics which is itself originally ethical, being constructed from its own material, the will, is the effective and immediate support of ethics...[25]

In this sense, there is a great change, since ethics, and consequently reason, are found in the individual. Therefore, it is safer to trust the individual than to rely on social structures. From here we can understand the moral law as opposed to

25 Arthur Schopenhauer, *Sobre a Vontade na Natureza*, trans. Gabriel Valladão Silva (Porto Alegre: L&PM editores, 2013), 209–210.

social law, which is, according to Rank, used by the groups in power. Therefore, moral law is "the expression of our moral self"[26], and as such it does not have to be imposed from the outside—it is self-imposed, aiming at the preservation of the person, both in the physical and symbolic aspects, and is present in the culture of the community. Further, we could add, moral law is pertinent to face-to-face relationships, or any close relations where consensus arises. On the other hand, social law is linked to social stratification and the asymmetry of power and is imposed on the individual from outside: "For the moral law from the beginning was common, that is, popular law, whereas social law was dictated by the group in power".[27]

Society, Heteronomy, and Autonomy

Given the foregoing, the exponent of moral law is the individual. It is here that the will is presented, and, expressing itself as an organism, it needs to be preserved. It is preserved not only in the physical aspect, but also in the symbolic aspect. The question that Rank presents to us is that, although the individual finds in culture a welcoming space for his or her project of development and expression, society, as a secondary group and detached from the individual, shows itself to be hostile, because society wants not creative expression but conformity. It is against society that the *artist*—the creative individual who affirms difference, that is, individuality, in a productive and constructive way—will fight the hardest struggle.

Therefore, society is not a reflection of moral law. Indeed, factors that deny individual autonomy, such as the need to assert some groups over others, the production of scapegoats, and the heroism that must be done against someone, have as their agent the asymmetry of power conditioned by social stratification that, according to Becker, accompanied the emergence of more complex societies and their social structures.

Likewise, primitive societies, little structured in terms of political organization, had mechanisms to prevent some person

26 Rank, 1958, 145–146.
27 Ibid., 146.

or group from accumulating a threatening amount of power. If asymmetry is not realized, the lesser conditions are that an individual may wish to assert his or her potency in the world by destroying another. In contemporary, highly stratified societies, the opposite occurs.

Moreover, Rank seems to add to this picture Nietzsche's skepticism in asserting that the so-called truths are at best metaphors, analogies, metonymies, and so on.

Although the pragmatic aspect of the first Nietzsche could see in this the value of an affirmation of potency, this affirmation could only be made from the individual, insofar as the organism that expresses the power necessarily is the individual. Therefore, to the extent that any narrative must believe in permanence, and consequently in being, that being that needs to be imagined is closer to the individual, which manifests potency by his or her own condition as an organism that has life.

However, if we are to affirm that moral law is *par excellence* of the individual, we seem to take from society what would be the greatest legitimation of its value, that is, of being the space of a law that imposes itself on the individual and would be, supposedly, morally legitimate. Indeed, Kant thought in this way in terms of civil society, which would ideally have the *republic* as the form of human beings, as beings endowed with rationality, organize themselves in a constructive way.[28] In the same way, social ordering had to follow a reason recognized by all the individual consciences, where it became autonomous, and therefore moral, insofar as it was accepted by the freedom of the will of beings who have the use of reason, for the sake of common good:

> As Hobbes asserts, the state of nature is a state of violence and arrogance and we must necessarily abandon it to submit to the coercion of laws, which does not limit our freedom but are able to reconcile with the freedom of any other, and thus with the common good. . .. this results from the original right of human reason to know no other

28 Immanuel Kant, *Filosofia da História*, trans. Cláudio J. A. Rodrigues (São Paulo: Ícone, 2012), 101.

> judge than the universal human reason itself, where each has its own voice; and, because of this, must come all the improvement of which our state is susceptible...[29]

Conclusion: Moral Law and Autonomy of the Individual

Kant has established that, in the world of phenomena, we cannot have contact with the thing in itself, although, when reason is alone in asking itself "how should I act?" it has direct contact with the intelligible world, which becomes, for the practical purposes of reason, the moral world. For these practical purposes, contact with moral law has more "truth" than contact with the phenomenon. Therefore, moral law, according to Kant, is no illusion. We must remember that, even if it is determined by something that does not generate sensible experience, thinking about it would present only speculation, since empirical data are not possible, and thus would be, concerning pure reason, useless. Thus, we see that this would be the moment when pure reason would produce illusions, just as in the past it produced old metaphysics. This Kantian approach is evident in Rank's thinking and gives fuller meaning to his work. Let's consider, in this context, this short passage from his book *Psychology and the Soul*:

> The human psychological universal that has been passed down is after all the soul, our soul-belief—the old psychology we believe in at heart but keep out of mind in modern psychology.
>
> This interpretation accords with the ethnological finding that unlike people with the "modern" world view, "primitives" are oriented toward a spiritual world, not one of reality. The laws of causality play a minor role in primitive mentality; the major role is played by all manner of celestial and supernatural forces that are not part of nature but are projected from self onto nature. As we have become more realistic, we have buried the soul deeper and deeper within, because there was no place for it in the external world. Unlike us, the first people acknowledged the soul, believed in it consciously, and filled the world with that soul-belief. They made the world less real, more

29 Kant, 2001, 616–617.

> like the self.[30]

How could a "less real" world be more faithful to the self? This is possible because, especially about the choices of the human being, this external reality is also made up of metaphors, analogies, and metonymies, and this is even more ethically significant insofar as these metaphors, analogies, and metonymies generate social stratification, exclusion, and scapegoats. To the extent that reality is at the service of the empowerment of some and the disempowerment of many, it plays a role in the asymmetry of power, and so, at least in terms of moral reason, it is not objective or "scientific," and it is even less neutral. It is fictional and is likely to be oriented to fulfill the role of victimizing those who have been elected by the hegemonic group to be the outcasts.

From the questioning of the young Nietzsche, Rank assumes that there is no "reality" in complete opposition to an "illusion." What is considered as reality is also a human construction, as well as being the material that is defined as what is known as the obstacle to the expression of being. In addition to this, we have the element of the production of asymmetry, in which the group that considers itself "the chosen ones" needs to disqualify the other groups and will often seek to destroy those non-elect.

With all this, reality, in the aspect of human choices, will be the illusion of the group in power that is imposed on the rest of society. In this way, it makes much more sense for the individual to follow the moral law that reason reveals within himself or herself. This moral law also consists of choices that cannot be verified in the empirical world, although they assert themselves as an affirmation of the values of the person, which, from that moment, are extended to the world so that the world is fulfilled with a human meaning, *from self onto the world*, in Rank's words.

Equally, it is possible to say that this inner certainty, in Rank's writings, becomes an affirmation of the values of the individual, and not an affirmation of the values of the broader society, in its political system, economic system, and so on.

30 Otto Rank, *Psychology and the Soul*, trans. Gregory C. Richter and E. James Lieberman (Baltimore: The John Hopkins University Press, 1998), 8.

Therefore, we must consider the implication that there is more coherence in the person living by his or her illusion than dying for the illusion of the socioeconomic system, for instance, in warfare. However, Rank could only establish this position insofar as he thought the individual to have an inner space of freedom, which we can understand as derived from Kant's moral philosophy. If it were not for this, the determinations that move the society, understood as the socioeconomic system, would also move the individual, who, in this paradigm, would have neither autonomy nor freedom. This inner space of will and ethics, made possible by a reason that in its practical aspect is autonomous, enables the values of the self to be present in the world, affirming the human meaning in the world:

> In a word, we encounter here for the first time the actual ground of psychology, the realm of willing and ethics in the purely psychic, not in the biological or [social] moral sense, therefore not in terms of any supra-individual force, but of freedom as Kant understood it metaphysically, that is, beyond external influences.[31]

31 Rank, 1978, 71.

Bibliography

Becker, Ernest, *La Estructura del Mal: Un Ensayo sobre la Unificación de la Ciencia del Hombre*. Translated by Carlos Valdés. México: Fondo de Cultura Económica, 1993.

—. *La Lucha Contra el Mal*. Translated by Carlos Valdés. México: Fondo de Cultura Económica, 1992.

Berger, Peter. L. and Luckmann, Thomas. *A Construção Social da Realidade*.

Translated by Floriano de Souza Fernandes. Petrópolis: Vozes, 1985.

Huizinga, Johan. *Homo Ludens*. Translated by João Paulo Monteiro. São Paulo: Perspectiva, 2000.

Kant, Immanuel. *Crítica da Razão Pura*. Translated by Manuela Pinto dos Santos and Alexandre Fradique Morujão. Lisbon: Calouste Gulbenkian, 2001.

—. *Filosofia da História*. Translated by Cláudio J. A. Rodrigues. São Paulo: Ícone, 2012.

Lieberman, E. James. *Acts of Will: The Life and Work of Otto Rank*. Amherst: University of Massachusetts Press, 1993.

Maffesoli, Michel. *O Tempo das Tribos: o Declínio do Individualismo nas Sociedades de Massa*. Translated by Maria de Lourdes Menezes. Rio de Janeiro: Forense Universitária, 1987.

Nietzsche, Friedrich. *Aurora*. Translated by Antônio Carlos Braga. São Paulo: Escala, 2007.

Rank, Otto. *Art and Artist*. Translated by Charles Francis Atkinson. New York: W.W. Norton & Company Inc., 1989.

—. *Beyond Psychology*. New York: Dover Publications Inc, 1958.

—. *Psychology and the Soul*. Translated by Gregory C. Richter and E. James Lieberman. Baltimore: The John Hopkins University Press, 1998.

—. *Truth and Reality*. Translated by Jessie Taft. New York: W.W. Norton & Company Inc., 1978.

Schopenhauer, Arthur. *O Mundo como Vontade e como Representação*. Translated by Jair Barboza. São Paulo: UNESP, 2005.

—. *Sobre a Vontade na Natureza*. Translated by Gabriel Valladão Silva. Porto Alegre: L&PM, 2013.

Silva, André Gustavo Ferreira and Luís Lucas Dantas da Silva. "Kant: A Formação Moral como uma Tarefa Histórica da Espécie Humana". *Espaço Pedagógico*, vol. 21, no. 1, (Passo Fundo: Jan./Jun. 2014), 132–145.

Solomon, Sheldon, Jeff Greenberg and Tom Pysczcynski. "Tales from the Crypt: on the Role of Death in Life." *Zygon*, vol. 33, no. 1 (Chicago, Illinois: March 1988), 9– 43.

Vaihinger, Hans. *A Filosofia do Como Se*. Translated by Johannes Kretschmer. Chapecó: Argos, 2011.

A Perspective on the Evolution of Psychoanalysis

Transcendence: A window of opportunity

Gary Kolb, PhD

Abstract

Human understanding is more complex than we believe. We continue to filter and transpose information in a manner that fits our needs. Accurate or not, we have had time to improvise and revisit past experiences with our interpretational point of view. Could there be something that we may be missing or misinterpreting when we engage in communication, especially from another's point of reference or even our own? In the field of psychoanalysis, this argument must be also addressed when considering the pathway of the future evolution of human connection.

Merleau-Ponty, a French philosopher, authored a detailed explanation of his understanding of transcendence and its effects on perception. Transcendence describes what lies beyond sense experience, but not beyond knowledge (Webster, 2005). Studying "Phenomenology of perception" (Merleau-Ponty, 2004) was initially quite challenging for this person trained and practicing in the field of psychology and psychoanalysis. The material was unfamiliar and in the beginning did not seem to have a practical use. However, transcendence may offer new insights into rudimentary elements of concepts that are often overlooked or viewed as commonplace material without adequate definition by psychologists. I found the concept of transcendence quite fascinating and definitely connected with my continuing interest in what may be left out of or skimmed over concepts involving a deeper understanding of the human connection. In fact, I believe that we often miss opportunities for a deeper connectedness by forcing our subjectivity onto what we perceive is an accurate perception from our senses of phenomena in life.

Case in point, when an analyst meets a client for the first time, the analyst is apt to force into his or her own subjective thoughts a preconceived notion of the client's operational behavior. This methodology often leads to distortion due to a faulty initial interpretation. Entry into this preconceived notion can take time for the analyst to sort out self-perpetuated beliefs. It also creates the possibility of internalizing a struggle for adequate awareness for a growing body of information for bench marks in future ongoing analytic material. Henceforth, I will introduce several concepts from Merleau-Ponty concerning the concept of Transcendence.

Merleau-Ponty (2004) believed that his life was always being thrown headlong into transcendent things and passed wholly outside of himself. He contended that this process of influence makes its way among objects without him needing to have them expressly in mind (p.429). According to Merleau-Ponty, his writing is not influenced by a certain set of ideas, but by

> an open situation, for which I could not possibly provide any situation, for which I could not possibly a provide any complex formula, and in which I struggle blindly on until miraculously, thoughts and words become organized by themselves (2004, p.429).

He suggested that environmental variables do not influence him, but that his consciousness "takes flight from itself" and in the environmental variables "is unaware of itself (2004, p.429). Realism tries to explain this by asserting an actual transcendence, and existence in itself of the world and ideas.

According to Merleau-Ponty (2004, p.430), transcendent things cannot be possessed by a person because a person is ignorant of what the transcendent things are, but acknowledges that these things exist. Merleau-Ponty (2004, p.430) proposed that experiencing a transcendent thing is possible only if its project is born and discovered within a person. He wrote that a person is capable of recognizing things around him by his actual contact with them. During contact with an object, a person's senses pick up information which the person utilizes to create a perception of the object. Then he contemplates how this object applies to himself and creates a personal knowledge or understanding of it. To describe an object situated in a subject's world, the person apparently must substitute a second variable by which it constructs or constitutes the world itself (Merleau-Ponty, 2004, p.431). This is especially true when the person's mind has already constructed a significant sign beforehand (2004, p.430). The second substitute is more authentic than the first because the transactions between the subject and the things around it are possible only if the subject causes them to exist for itself, arranges them around itself, and extracts them from its own core (2004, p.431).

Merleau-Ponty (2004) described how a person understands his or her environment. The process begins when the person picks up information through his or her senses. The person perceives something of interest and creates a cognito or thought about it. The person thinks about how this information applies to him and builds a personal knowledge of understanding of the thing of interest. The Cartesian cogito (self-awareness) is always beyond what it brings to mind at the moment (2004, p.431) and only becomes significant through a person's own cogito. It is the person who assigns thought to the object and constantly verifies thought orientation toward this objective (2004, p.431). Merleau-Ponty suggested that

> unless thought itself had put into things what it subsequently finds in them, it would have no hold upon them and would be an illusion of thought (2004, p.432).

According to Merleau-Ponty, all of our experiences and reflections are rooted in a being that immediately recognizes itself and knows its own existence by having direct contact with it (2004, p.432). He describes self-consciousness as "the very being of mind in action" (2004, p.432).The act of self-consciousness must be caught at the moment it occurs, before it collapses (2004, p.432).

Merleau-Ponty wrote that "the Cartesian doctrine of the cogito logically leads to the timelessness of mind and to accepting a consciousness of the external" (2004, p.433). Eternity can be understood as the power to embrace and anticipate temporal developments in a single intention which is the definition of subjectivity. Cogito is presented in terms of eternity. It is timeless and includes the perception discovering oneself as the universal constituent of all being accessible to the person and as a transcendental field without hidden corners and no outside (Merleau-Ponty, 2004, p.433). It includes the form of all objects of sense. The mind eludes the outside spectator and can only be recognized from within the person's cogito (2004, p.434). The mind is unique to the person and cannot be shared with anyone else. However, Merleau-Ponty wondered if the mind could be transferable to another (2004, p.434). It is not precisely understood how the world comes to belong to the subject and the subject to himself which is what makes experience, our hold on things, and on our states of consciousness possible (2004, p.435). Merleau-Ponty maintained that consciousness is transcendence through and through. The cogito is "a deep-seated momentum of transcendence which is my very being, the simultaneous contact with my own being and with the world's being" (2004, p.438-439).

To be effective, a therapist or analyst needs to recognize the role the cognito plays in the counseling or psychoanalytic process. Both the therapist's cognito and the client's cognito are involved. Since a cognito is formed from information from the senses and is based on personal experience, it can never be completely accurate. When two people witness the same event, for example an accident, they will not report exactly the same information about it. Each person's cognito contains some element of illusion or distortion. This is also true in a counseling situation. The therapist becomes the subject and the client the object.

The therapist attempts to understand the client's issues and forms a cognito concerning the client which may not be completely accurate. The therapist looks for an adequate understanding of the client, while the client searches for interpretation and understanding about him or herself. People tend to communicate in illusory ways, so the therapist attempts to discern from what the client reveals what is protection, what is false interpretation, and what is reality. The client is not necessarily being deceptive in his or her communication, since protection and false interpretation result from the natural way a person processes information. The therapist is trained to listen for symbolism, distortion, and commonality. The therapist attempts to decode the illusion in what the client says. Transcendence is always present.

Conclusion

This paper only offers a thought as to a deeper search for meaning of the human mind. It is intended to offer a resurrected perspective to understanding the mind and how it inter-intra relates in human communication. This view may be looked as a new exploration for the analyst's consideration in understanding the client. As we move into a faster paced society, we are integrating the evolutional development of technology into our human relatedness. Although the philosophical perspective is an older base point of reference to understanding the human connection, it also continues to offer a new perspective on the way we approach human communication, understanding, and knowledge.

References

1. Ponty, Merleau, (2004) Phenomenology of Perception. London and New York: Rutledge Classics.

2. Webster Dictionary (2005) Webster's School & Office Dictionary. New York: Federal Street Press

Adorno and the Problem of Systematicity

Daniel Green, PhD Candidate

Key words: Critical Theory, Adorno, Nietzsche, Art, Systematicity, Ideology, Culture, Negative Dialectics

Abstract

The purpose of this paper is twofold: first, to argue that Adorno is one of the few to answer Nietzsche's call to a philosophical revolution; and second, that if we view Adorno in this way, as a disciple of Nietzsche, it will aid in refuting the common criticism of Adorno that he fails at his critical project because of his lack of systematicity.

In the first argument, I will establish Adorno's criticism of traditional metaphysics. This criticism argues that systematic philosophy, or what Adorno often refers to as idealism (probably with the German Idealists in mind), attempts to build an explanation that can exhaustively explain all of reality. Adorno argues that due to the ever changing and heterogeneous nature of reality, this project is impossible. This is because the generalizing tools that philosophy makes use of, such as words, concepts, and systems cannot capture the varied nature of reality. Thus, Adorno argues, these philosophers' motivation must be something other than truth, it must be a craving for control and certainty.

I will illustrate how this view answers Nietzsche's claims at the beginning of *Beyond Good and Evil*, that metaphysics has always been motivated by subconscious desires that philosophers' have chosen to ignore. Or, in other words, that the Will to Truth is in fact deluded, for nobody is ever aiming at impersonal truth but looking for some personal gain. Adorno takes this challenge a step further and illustrates how these subconscious, hidden, motivations keep us from being free. He then carves out a new role for philosophy that can free us from these subconscious patterns. Finally I hope this argument, that Adorno's view of philosophy is a practical application of Nietzsche, will dispel criticisms of Adorno for being unsystematic. For if we are to take Nietzsche seriously, to be systematic, to claim to have the truth, would be to ignore the subconscious motivations for our actions. Thus, in taking Nietzsche seriously, Adorno must carve out a new, unsystematic role for philosophy.

Introduction

In the first section of his work *Beyond Good and Evil*, Nietzsche poses a challenge to philosophy that, if taken seriously, would drastically change the methodology, aims, and the very intention for undertaking philosophical work. The main challenge Nietzsche ushers to philosophy consists in an unveiling of what he believes actually underlies what he calls the "Will to Truth." Philosophers traditionally have engaged in metaphysics in order to arrive at the true ontological make up of reality. A successful metaphysical picture would be objective, universal, and impersonal. It would in no way be influenced by the particular constitution of the philosopher, for then it would not apply to the whole of reality. Nietzsche questions this impersonal nature of metaphysics. He writes, "The greater part of the conscious thinking of a philosopher is secretly influenced by his instincts, and forced into definite channels. And behind all logic and its seeming sovereignty of movement, there are valuations, or to speak more plainly, physiological demands, for the maintenance of a definite mode of life" (Nietzsche, 4). Here, Nietzsche points to the impurity hiding within the motivation to practice metaphysics, within the Will to Truth. The fault of the metaphysicians of the past lies in their inability to pierce beyond the surface of the mind. What manifests at the surface of the mind, in conscious thinking, as conceptual or logical truth seeking, is actually motivated by an instinctual drive for a certain way of living. As he later writes, "Indeed to understand how the abstrusest metaphysical assertions of a philosopher have been arrived at it is always well (and wise) to ask: What morality do they aim at?" (Nietzche, 5). If we take Nietzsche seriously there are no pure truth claims. To view a metaphysical claim as merely an explanation of the world would be to ignore the depths of the mind, which contain the true motivation for any truth claim, a drive for a certain way of being. Thus, if Nietzsche is correct, all philosophy, or at least all metaphysics, is and has been but an expression of the ethical dispositions or subconscious desires of particular philosophers.

Clearly, accepting Nietzsche's challenges to philosophy is a tall order. These challenges ask us to reassess everything we know about the motivation and the purposes for undertaking a philosophical project. Thus, while some thinkers have worked with Nietzsche's insights, many have ignored them or brushed them over, continuing the pursuit of "truth." One philosopher who I will argue has taken Nietzsche very seriously is Theodor Adorno. More specifically, I believe we can look at Adorno's outline of the function of philosophy as an attempt to not just take Nietzsche seriously, but also as a way of applying Nietzsche's ideas in a practical way. Adorno applies Nietzsche's claims to a practical project: liberation from cultural coercion. He shows us how surface level philosophical or metaphysical claims conceal habitual patterns of cultural conditioning. Adorno also suggests that if we can use philosophy to reveal these concealed aspects of experience, rather than cover them over, we can use it to liberate us from this conditioning. Looking at Adorno's view of philosophy as an application of Nietzsche's ideas will have two main benefits. First, it will be helpful in understanding Adorno's project and his new task for philosophy, and second it will make sense of, and I believe, dispel the main criticism of Adorno, that he is not "systematic" enough, or never comes up with a final theory or framework.[1]

Adorno on Theoretical Philosophy

Before we can sufficiently argue that Adorno's view of philosophy is an answer to Nietzsche's criticism, we must have an in depth picture of his philosophy itself, both at the theoretical level, what exactly philosophy is for Adorno, and at the practical level, in what ways it can be used to liberate us from cultural coercion. To get an initial feel for Adorno's conception of of philosophy, we can turn to his explanation of music and the analogy he draws between the structure of the two. He writes, "In music the impulse animating the first bar

1 For examples of this specific criticism see Rudiner Bunber's Habermas' Concept of Critical Theory, Adorno and Mead: Micheal Hoover's Toward an Interactionist Critique of Negative Dialectics, and Peter Hohendal's The Dialectic of Enlightenment Revisited: Habermas' Critique of the Frankfurt School

will not be fulfilled at once but only in further articulation... music is a critique of phenomenality, of the appearance that the substance is present here and now. Such a mediate role befits philosophy no less" (Adorno 16). A musical piece is never complete in the present moment. What is graspable never exhausts the musical experience. This is because music is a movement. The piece always extends to what it is not; yet that future that it has not been or the past which it was before are still intimately related in some way to what we are currently experiencing. Similarly, for Adorno, philosophy must be a movement, like music, it can never be "complete," at one instant in time. It must constantly respond to new information that we receive as our present experience unfolds in unpredictable ways. As we will see in more detail in the following section, traditional systematic philosophical thought cannot accomplish this task because it does not stay open to changing experience. Rather, the traditional philosophical system takes a set of concepts as exhaustive in the explanation of the world and thus they act as a filter. All experience is filtered through these concepts and if there are certain bits of information which cannot fit within this particular conceptual scheme, they get repressed or ignored. For this reason, philosophy must always remain malleable and never complete. In Adorno's own words, "Its' course must be a ceaseless self-renewal, by its own strength as well as in friction with whatever standard it may have. The crux is what happens in it, not a thesis or position" (Adorno 33). As we will see in more detail later, for Adorno, any type of final, fixed view is a bondage, for it necessarily obscures the changing nature of reality. To be free is to be in line with this ever changing nature as best we can. Philosophy must be a process, for getting stuck in a concept, or in a system, will only increase the weight of our bondage.

Adorno's Opponent: Idealism or the System

Some questions may arise at this point; how can one do philosophy in a non systematic way? Is not the nature of philosophy to explain the world in a positive sense? Do not the very tools philosophy uses, words and concepts, suggest a rigidity of explanation? These questions will be addressed in the sections below. We can begin the process by looking to what Adorno says specifically concerning his opponent:

systematic philosophy, or what he often refers to as idealism. Of the philosophical system, Adorno writes, "Every system was such an order, such an absurdly rational product: a positive thing posing being-in-itself. Its origin had to be placed into formal thought divorced from content; nothing else would let it control material" (Adorno 21). Here, Adorno points out two important qualities of the philosophical system, one that it is merely formal, and two, that as a merely formal system, it stands independent of any content in the real world which may have spurred its creation. To understand this one may consider certain systems of mathematics. Initially, they can be seen as mapping and categorizing objects found in concrete experience. We see a number of similar objects, put them in one to one correspondence with certain signs, and call these numbers. Manipulating these numbers can help us understand how to manipulate the objects in certain ways. However, as this system of numbers become more and more abstract, let's say we start adding in negative numbers, and infinity, it starts to become more difficult to locate the link to our actual experience. Systematic philosophy for Adorno is similar, it may start grounded in dynamic, lived experience, but it eventually runs away with itself, multiplying itself through leaps of logic that reference only components within the system itself.

We next come to Adorno's last comment in this quote, "nothing else will let it control material." Here, we can remember Nietzsche's suggestion that subconscious motivations underly all metaphysical claims. Adorno asks us to look for what the hidden motivation for creating such a formal system could be. He claims that the motivation for creating such a philosophy is not truth or liberation but rather control. To further explain this point Adorno actually cites Nietzsche. He writes, "According to Nietzsche's critique, systems no longer documented anything but the finickiness of scholars compensating themselves for political impotence by conceptually construing their, so to speak, administrative authority over things in being" (Adorno 20). The motivation for the conceptual or formal system is a desire for control. The philosopher describes the world with concepts that she can understand and make sense of. Thus, if this system and these concepts are taken as encompassing all of reality, the philosopher can rest content, knowing that nothing lies beyond her grasp. She believes she has nullified the danger of unpredictability in life by fitting all that she experiences into her formal filter. As Adorno writes elsewhere, "Whenever something that is to be conceived flees from identity with the concept, the concept will be forced to take exaggerated steps to prevent any doubts of the unassailable validity, solidity and acribia of the thought product from stirring" (Adorno 22). We can look at the motivation for idealism as a type of neuroticism of identity, an attempt to pin down a world and an identity which is stable, which is "mine." Of course, to liberate ourselves from our bondages, we must truly understand them, not hide them underneath metaphysical concepts. So we must always be on the watch for new forms these bondages may mask themselves as. For this purpose, a system that reinterprets differences as the same, and blocks out new information, trying to force it again and again into the same mold will not do. We need a method of philosophy which is open ended and attentive to change in form, constantly reassessing.

Adorno's Positive View

As one may predict given his caution when engaging with systematic thought and exhaustive explanations, Adorno's positive view is less a philosophical system itself and more the carving out of a new role for philosophy. We see that Adorno is critical of philosophy as a cohesive, constructive force, a type of world builder. He writes, "Criticism of systems and asystematic thought are superficial as long as they cannot release the cohesive force which the idealistic system had signed over to the transcendental subject" (Adorno 26). Adorno suggests here that philosophy traditionally gives the power of world creation to the transcendental subject. As an example of this we can look to Kant and his "I think," which builds the world through the Forms of the Intuition. For Kant, some transcendental subject uses certain logical forms to turn the manifold of sensation into a comprehensible, intelligible world. In more simple language, the subject uses certain logical relations to build a world out of a formless mass of stimuli. For the systematic idealists such as Kant, concepts or logical relations, whose meaning are taken at face value and completely given for the subject, structure the world. This leaves reality easily accessible, explainable, and identifiable for any subject who cares to engage in conceptual analysis. However, Adorno wants to point to a new world "glue" by which the world is constructed. He writes,

> "To change this direction of conceptuality, to give it a turn towards nonidentity, is the hinge of negative dialectics. Insight into the constitutive character of the nonconceptual in the concept would end the compulsive identification which the concept brings unless halted by reflection. Reflection upon its own meaning is the way out of the concept's seeming being-in-itself as a unit of meaning." (Adorno 12).

Here, Adorno is suggesting that the view of the system or the concept as constructive of a completely transparent, understandable world is an illusion. This becomes clear as we look at the nature of the concept, or what Adorno refers to as its "constitutive character," its origin. We further see that true insight into this "constitutive character" will take a turn towards nonidentity and will reveal the falsity of looking at the concept as a "being-in-itself" as a unit of meaning. Or more simply put, it will reveal the impossibility of taking the concept at face value. A simple way to understand this is that the concept is not transparent, we can never grasp it all it once, because it is partly constituted by that which exceeds our grasp. Once we understand its true constitution we will see that by its very nature, the concept cannot save the philosopher from her fear of nonidentity. In other words, philosophy's true role cannot be constructive, it cannot be to reveal to us the structure of the world.

To understand why philosophy's role must be something other than a revelation of the true world for Adorno, we must understand in depth why it is the case that any concept or system cannot totally reveal the world's structure to us. We must delve into this idea that the concept always contains that which it cannot express. Adorno writes, "The double meaning of philosophical systematics leaves no choice but to transpose the power of thought, once delivered from the systems into the open realm of definition by individual moments" (Adorno 25). Here, Adorno comments that in order for philosophy to succeed we must move away from the idea that the transparent definition, the concept, governs thought. We must realize that it is "individual moments" that have the true power. I believe the way we can understand these "individual moments" and how they relate to the birth of the concept is quite simple. Individual moments can be seen as direct experience; sensation, feeling, drives, a seething mass of desires etc. (what exactly this preconceptual experience consists in is a whole different philosophical discussion) The concept is used to categorize these experiences by fitting qualitatively different experiences into general groups by which they can be called the same. For example, I may call all emotional experiences that lead to passionate outbursts anger, even though all these experiences have different bodily sensational content. Thus, the concept has the result of monotonizing experience, making the different into the same. At the theoretical level, this monotonization occurs because there is no true symmetry between these individual moments and the system or the concept. The system cannot be a substitute for the them. The concept seeks to generalize and the object, or experience, is heterogeneous. This leads to a necessary gap between explanation, which always works in generalizations, and that which is being explained, which is always specific and never general. Thus, a philosophical system must always leave out bits of information, it necessarily creates a gap or an asymmetry between its explanation of reality and reality itself. It is for this reason, as we saw earlier, that metaphysical systems often run away with themselves, and cease to refer to anything in the actual world, discussing only their own formal content.

Adorno's Practical Project

Before we can truly see what role Adorno has for philosophy other than this, in his opinion, futile constructive project, we must also get a sense for his practical picture, what a genuine philosophical work may look like and how it would liberate us from cultural coercion. We have seen that for Adorno, the comprehensible world is built through inaccurate generalizations. These generalizations are what keep us from being free and can manifest in a number of ways. At a personal, non theoretical level these generalizations manifest as learned responses to stimuli that have been ingrained in us by what Adorno commonly refers to as "The Culture Industry." We can look at an obvious example, advertisements. If we are particularly susceptible to television commercials, and we constantly see a commercial of people wearing Old Navy jeans who are happy and healthy; whenever we go to the store and see those jeans on sale, that feeling will arise in us. Quite possibly without even being aware of it, we will buy those jeans because they have conditioned within us that expectation of happiness and health. Of course, Old Navy jeans are not going to bring us any kind of lasting happiness or health. This is just an ingrained, irrational, very likely subconscious habit pattern. This is a very gross example, but hopefully we can see the similarity to systematic philosophy, another way in which these generalizations can manifest. Let's say we are Hegelians, and are convinced that everything is Absolute Spirit. Initially when we are convinced of Hegel's point we may come to some wonderful, mystical, feeling of the connectedness of all things. Then let us say we leave our office, get in our car and someone cuts us off. Anger arises, yet we tell ourselves, don't worry this person is also Absolute Spirit, that mystical feeling comes back and represses the anger. Of course, this also is a simplistic example, but like this, systematic philosophy can be used to actually drown out reality. By connecting certain concepts with certain feelings through conditioning, we apply these concepts to the endless variety of experiences of life, homogenize them, and repress or ignore how we actually feel or how things actually appear, in favor of the security of categorizing them under a familiar concept.

The role for philosophy for Adorno then cannot be a constructive role, it cannot build a world, because to build an identity which extends over space and time is to limit and ignore the ever changing nature of space and time. Philosophy must be able to fight both these forms of subconscious conditioning and repression, personal, as with the advertisements, and conceptual, as with systematic philosophy. To see how this can be done let us look to a quotation. What philosophy can do, Adorno calls reconcilement. Of this he writes,

> As the subject-object dichotomy is brought to mind it becomes inescapable for the subject, furrowing whatever the subject thinks, even objectively-but it would come to

> an end in reconcilement. Reconcilement would release the nonidentical, would rid it of coercion, including spiritualized coercion, it would open the road to the multiplicity of different things and strip dialectics of its power over them...Dialectics serves the end of reconcilement (Adorno 6).

Here, Adorno points out the only possible solution to this puzzle. If the concept or the system is necessary to hold the subject up as in individual existent, then, to reach what is beyond the concept and to stay with "the multiplicity of different things", the subject must be dissolved. Adorno calls this dissolution of the subject/object distinction reconcilement and names it the goal of Negative Dialectics, his name for this new method of philosophy. Through reconcilement we reach the heterogeneous which is unidentifiable, and we free ourselves from the tyranny of systematic philosophy and of cultural conditioning, which both constantly yet futily try to categorize reality into something we can exhaustively comprehend. Thus, philosophy must serve a deconstructive purpose rather than a constructive purpose. It must reveal the contradiction which lies within any system or any explanation.

Reconcilement: A Phenomenological Picture of the role of Philosophy for Adorno

In parts of his paper *The Culture Industry*, Adorno parallels for art what the introduction of *Negative Dialectics* does for philosophy. He outlines how art usually functions to propagate ideology, and then carves out a new, critical role for art. The main difference is that in this paper, Adorno moves away from the purely theoretical and describes what kind of direct experience could lead to reconcilement and what this process would look like. Thus, I believe an exploration of the experience induced by a truly critical work of art will be helpful for getting a concrete phenomenological picture of how reconcilement could be achieved.

Adorno describes traditional artistic pieces as based on a harmonious, unified style. However, the problem with this "feel good" type of art is that it ends up harmonizing the subject with the specific coercive patterns of the time period. For example, Adorno writes, "The unity of style not only of the Christian Middle Ages but of the Renaissance expresses the different structures of social coercion in those periods" and more generally, "By claiming to anticipate fulfillment through aesthetic derivatives, it posits the real forms of the existing order as absolute. To this extent the claims of art are always also ideology." (Adorno 103). Here, we see that the hidden function of this work of art is to harmonize us with the existing social order. The work of art which unifies style, which harmonizes, and makes us feel good does all this within the context of our current, comfortable, yet socialized identity. An example of this could be pop music in a club setting. Social coercion has influenced us to think that to have fun we must go pay exorbitantly expensive cover charges at clubs and buy equally expensive drinks. When we get into the club we hear some rap song where the artist raps about how much fun they are having in the club. The rapper may be technically skilled and the beat may be harmonious. Thus, the song affirms these ideological behaviors by pairing them with aesthetically beautiful elements. Our socially constructed identities are reified through artistic experience.

Hopefully, we can see the parallel here to Adorno's view of traditional philosophy. Just as the stylized, harmonious, work of art reifies our socially constructed identity, the philosophical system does the same. When we identify with a certain philosophical system or set of concepts, we become complacent in the identity which these suggest. Thus, as Hegelians, we can rest content knowing that we really are Absolute Spirit, or as Fichteans that we really are the Absolute I. Sufficiently comforted and numbed by these concepts, we can absentmindedly settle into a set of behavior patterns given to us by The Culture Industry.

If the ideological work of art harmonizes us with a socially constructed sense of identity, then the true work of art must challenge that sense of identity. As we have seen the "feel good" elements of art are not capable of this. They make us happy, complacent, and affirm the comfortable, coerced behavior patterns by ennobling them with a beat. a rhythm, or some other pleasant aesthetic element. Thus, Adorno writes, "The moment in the work of art which transcends reality...does not consist in achieved harmony, in the questionable unity of form and content, inner and outer, individual and society, but in those traits in which the discrepancy emerges, in the necessary failure of the passionate striving for identity" (Adorno 103). The true work of art is not harmonious, is not aesthetically pleasing. The music that pleases the ear tells us that all is as it should be, everything is in order. However, real art wants to tell us viscerally that something is wrong, that somewhere in our identity there is a contradiction, a disharmony; essentially, that the striving for harmony between self and society, between subject and object, the striving for identity at all is a failed project from the start. For examples of this type of art let us look at how most music that is pleasing to the ear works. Usually a certain chord progression is associated with a certain emotion. So notes are strung together into a progression that stimulates the rising and falling of a particular emotion. In the genuine work of art, notes would not be strung together in a traditional progression. Maybe this work of art would take one note from the progression that usually induces joy, one from the sadness progression, one from the fear progression, and string them right in a row. Thus, the listener has no usual emotional reference points for interpreting this experience. She has no choice but to be with her visceral response as best she can, without categorizing or understanding it, because it is so unusual. We see this genuine work of art is unpleasant, is abrasive, it clashes with our structured way of interpreting the world. By conditioning an experience that cannot fit into our comfortable habits, that we cannot narrativize into our personal world systems, this work of art shows us that these comfortable systems and these identities are ultimately illusory.

Just as the ingenuine work of art had significant similarities to systematic philosophy, the genuine work of art is very similar to Adorno's view of true philosophy. Real art must always be negative, must always provide us with an experience that is so jarring and alien that it cannot be fit into our identities and socially constructed habit patterns. It reveals aspects of experience which were repressed or brushed over by our conditioning. Adorno's method of negative dialectics must do the same. Although we cannot say exactly what this type of philosophy would look like, for what serves the end of reconcilement will be contingent on a particular time and a particular space, we can point to how this work of philosophy may look. Again we can use the example of an unnatural chord progression. What philosophy usually does is establish conceptual reference points. It tells us that this particular phenomena means this, this other phenomena means this, and this is how they are connected. Just as an unnatural chord progression may force us to experience a type of emotion we cannot categorize, real philosophy must break down, or show us the illusory nature of these connections and categorizations and force us to experience a reality which we cannot categorize or explain.[2] Both real philosophy and real art must serve the end of reconcilement, of the breaking down of the harmony of dualities: subject/object, individual/society, inner/outer, to name a few. While the stylistic work of art and the systematic philosophical system affirm these dualities and try to point to a harmony between the two, Negative Dialectics and its artistic counterpart show the futility of this project by making clear there is always an experience or a component of the system which eludes any sort of identification or systemization. Thus, philosophy, if successful, ends in a type of existential death; one sees the impossibility of one's identity, one's world picture, and it crumbles; bringing down with it all the ideology which it was based on.

Adorno, Nietzsche, and Anti-Systematicity

This view of philosophy as a destruction of identity leads to an implication which is new for philosophy as a discipline. Under this picture, philosophy is never finished. Philosophy cannot be a truth or a system arrived at, but must be a process of negative response to the social and ideological condition at the time. We need only look to history to see that this is true. As a new order arises, it get incorporated back into the mainstream. For example, the counterculture of the 60's arose. Yet by the 70's psychedelic imagery was used for capitalist ends,

2 Examples of this type of philosophy are few and far between. It would also take a good bit of argumentation to illustrate that any work does in fact fall into this category. That being said, I believe a few promising places to look are Adorno's Negative Dialectics, Nietzsche's *Thus Spoke Zarathustra*, Heidegger's *Being and Time*, and Wittgenstein's *Philosophical Investigations*

placed on products to make them seem hip. Similarly, a work of philosophy may initially be revolutionary, be alive. At one moment in time It may reveal hidden motivations and habits in us which we before did not allow ourselves to see. However, over time this new identity, this new system will solidify and become stale, lifeless. We will need to see things from a fresh perspective once again. Of course, we cannot throw out systems and conceptual analysis completely, for we need structure to exist as subjects and get about in the world. However, the system must never be final, it must stay open to constant change. For even if our philosophy is successful, reconciliation is reached, and identity is annihilated, a new one must spring up; for we need dualities, we need subject and objects in order to have a world at all. Thus, once the new world, the new identity, and the new ideology is born, philosophy begins again within this new structure to break this down as well.

Adorno's view is often criticized on these grounds, that he views philosophy as purely negative, as Critical Theory scholar Bunber puts it, "never lays claim to theoretical status" (Bunber 44). There is no theory here, no set of standards which critics and philosophers alike can work with, no real progress, just an arguably pessimistic picture of a, maybe noble, yet endless struggle against the relentless forces of coercion and ideology. Adorno sought to free us from cultural coercion, critics say, yet failed. He was not able to provide us with a standard or set of standards by which we can always critique culture and thus clearly see where our bondages lie. It is in this spirit, that the next generation Critical Theorist, Jurgen Habermas, comes up with the Ideal Speech Situation. We will not go into the details of this theory here. It will suffice to say that for Habermas, the Ideal Speech Situation serves as an a priori standard by which we can judge every situation. If the situation meets this standard, the participants were acting in an uncoerced way, free of any hidden conditioning. If not, we must work to meet this standard. We see Adorno has no standard or system such as this. So how can we use his thinking to free ourselves?

If we look at Adorno as expanding on Nietzsche's project, we will see the fallacy of this criticism. To summarize, Nietzsche believes that metaphysical claims or systematic philosophy have not really been motivated by a pure Will to Truth, but rather by subconscious intentions for certain ways of being, or certain comfortable identities. Similarly, Adorno takes the motivations for most of our actions as hidden from our conscious mind. Cultural conditioning associates certain responses with certain general categories of stimuli. However, these responses are artificial and tend to gloss over or repress actual experience. So, at the surface, though it may seem that buying a new pair of jeans is making us happy, this is only a constructed, artificial response, covering up an ocean of sensations and emotions occurring at the depth of the mind. Systematic philosophy, for Adorno, serves this same end of covering up the deeper truth. It uses broad conceptual claims to generalize over a varied, ever changing experience, hiding us from the truth of transience. Thus, for Adorno, cultural conditioning and systematic philosophy work together in different spheres to make experience digestible but monotonous, comprehensible but shallow.

We see that if Adorno was to systematize, to set up some consistent standard like the Ideal Speech Situation, he would be ignoring Nietzsche's insight. He would be explaining only the workings of the surface of the mind, not penetrating the depths of subconscious motivations and conditioning. This would be to mistake neurotic craving for stability and consistency for transcendental truth. Adorno does not want to solidify and normalize these subconscious motivations but wants to reveal them. Furthermore, as we have seen, once they are exposed, they come back in a new form. Thus philosophy must be a process, it must never be final, constantly searching for the new forms these intentions may be hiding under.

Conclusion

In Nietzsche's work, *Thus Spoke Zarathustra*, Zarathustra is a wise prophetic figure. He has amassed a band of followers who hope to absorb some of Zarathustra's wisdom. At one point Zarathustra banishes these followers saying,

> Verily, I advise you: depart from me, and guard yourselves against Zarathustra! And better still: be ashamed of him! Perhaps he hath deceived you. The man of knowledge

> must be able not only to love his enemies, but also to hate his friends. One requiteth a teacher badly if one remain merely a student. And why will ye not pluck at my wreath? Ye venerate me; but what if your veneration should some day collapse? Take heed lest a statue crush you! Ye say, ye believe in Zarathustra? But of what account is Zarathustra! Ye are my believers: but of what account are all believers! Ye had not yet sought yourselves: then did ye find me. So do all believers; therefore all belief is of so little account. Now do I bid you lose me and find yourselves; and only when ye have all denied me, will I return unto you. (Nietzsche, 113).

In the spirit of Adorno as one of the few true disciples of Nietzsche, we can look at any philosophical system as Zarathustra encourages his followers to look at himself. No matter how much wisdom or truth the system contains, it means nothing if one has not done the work of criticism themselves. The goal of philosophy is not to arrive eternally at some truth, for this is to stagnate. Rather, it is to remain engaged in an endless project of self analysis and self criticism; again and again bringing to the surface the hidden depths of reality. This is really the spirit Adorno is trying to keep alive. He is telling us to always be skeptical, always be critical, even of our own conclusions. What liberated us one day may be hiding some unknown conditioning or motivation the next. Thus, we must constantly be on the watch, not condemning philosophy, but never letting it be finalized. Adorno urges us to use philosophy in the best way we can, even as a generalizing force, to be more open to the multiplicity of life, and to reveal pieces of that multiplicity that, remaining hidden, have kept us from true liberation.

Works Cited

Adorno, Theodor W., and E. B. Ashton. *Negative Dialectics.* New York: Seabury, 1979. Print.

Habermas, Jurgen. *Knowledge and Human Interests: A General Perspective.*

Bunber, Rudiger. *Habermas's Concept of Critical Theory.*

Nietzsche, Friedrich. *Beyond Good and Evil.* Translated by Helen Zimmern, Emereo, 2009.

Nietzsche, Friedrich. *Thus Spoke Zarathustra a Book for All an None.* Translated by Walter Kaufman, The Viking Press, 1970.

Adorno, T. & Horkheimer, M., 1944. *The Culture Industry: Enlightenment as Mass Deception.* T. Adorno and M. Horkheimer. Dialectics of Enlightenment. Translated by John Cumming. New York: Herder and Herder, 1972.

Back Page

In
Praise
Of Air

I write in praise of air. I was six or five
when a conjurer opened my knotted fist
and I held in my palm the whole of the sky.
I've carried it with me ever since.

Let air be a major god, its bein
and touch, its breast-milk always tilted
to the lips. Both dragonfly and Boening
dangle in its see-through nothingness…

Among the jumbled bric-a-brac I keep
a padlocked treasure-chest of empty space,
and on days when thoughts are fuddled with smog
or civilization crosses the street

with a white handkerchief over its mouth
and cars blow kisses to our lips from theirs
I turn the key, throw back the lid, breathe deep.
My first word, everyone's first word, was air.

Simon Armitage

The world's first catalytic poem developed in collaboration
with Professor Tony Ryan at the University of Sheffield.
Catalyticpoetry.org

Presencing EPIS

EPIS Journal Guidelines for Submission

Publication Details

Published by The Existential Psychoanalytic Institute & Society. One issue per year. Aims and Scope: Presencing EPIS is a scholarly, peer-reviewed journal dedicated to contemporary psychoanalysis. The journal covers theoretical and clinical issues emerging from existential psychoanalysis, phenomenology, traditional psychoanalysis, cultural studies, Critical Theory, post-structuralism, deconstruction, and fictional literature. The journal covers substantive and methodological issues in psychoanalysis and psychoanalytic psychotherapy, including ethical, political, professional, sociological, and historical ideas, especially as they relate to similar professional practice. Articles address theory, method, clinical case studies, previous articles, and research. The journal also has a book review and forum section for critical commentary on the journal itself.

Instructions for Authors

Papers may be theoretical, clinical, empirical, or methodological, between 2,500-7,500 words. Book reviews are up to 2,000 words and letters to the editor no more than 1,000 words. Presencing EPIS welcomes manuscripts from any country although the official language of the journal is English. All contributions will be anonymously reviewed, either by members of the Editorial Board or by panels of Independent Reviewers drawn from practitioners, researchers, academics or others who have made significant contributions to the field.

Decisions regarding publication will be made by the Editors with advice from the Editorial Board or Independent Reviewers with feedback provided to authors on decisions made. Editors can be contacted by potential contributors wishing to discuss a proposal or seeking advice or guidance on preparation of a submission.

Guidelines for Manuscripts

Manuscripts must be double-spaced on 8.5 x 11 inch pages, allowing for 1 inch minimum margins. The word count should be stated. The title should be brief and indicate the main topic of the article. A list of up to eight keywords should be supplied, as well as a summary abstract of up to 150 words. Names of authors should be given in full on a separate sheet. Authors should provide brief details (up to 50 words) of professional autobiography. Please include address, telephone, fax, and email as well. Where there are two or more authors, please indicate a single contact for correspondence.

Guidelines for Book Reviews

The main theme should be clearly presented but it is not the purpose of a review to summarize the book. Reviews should evaluate the book in relation to other significant work on the subject. Reviewers should assess the book the author has written rather than use the review as a vehicle for their own opinions, and should include criticisms with reference to specific instances in the text wherever possible. Apart from minor editions the Reviews Editor will not alter or cut without prior consultation with the reviewer. The invitation to review a book, however, does not constitute a guarantee that the manuscript will be published. To submit a book review or a book to be reviewed, please contact the Reviews Editor. Referencing Books and Articles: Use Either the Chicago Manual of Style or the APA depending upon your professional affiliation. Only works actually cited in the text should be included in the references. Indicate in the text by putting inside brackets the author's name and year of publication. References should be listed in alphabetical order at the end of the article. Publications from the same author in a single year should use a, b, c, and so forth.

Footnotes and Tables

Footnotes are not normally permitted but endnotes may be used if necessary. Tables should be Word objects, delineated clearly and supplied on separate pages, with an indication within the text of their approximate location. Vertical lines should be omitted and horizontal lines limited to those indicating the top and bottom of the table, below column headings and above summed totals. Totals and percentages should be labeled clearly. Guidelines for Graphic Images: Graphic images must be of professional quality and included as separate high-resolution files. Each image must be attached and named chronologically "figure 1," "figure 2," etc. Images must not be embedded in the manuscript itself. The approximate location of each image should be indicated in the manuscript with a stand-alone sentence: "Figure 1 approximately here," etc. Acceptable file formats: Word Documents preferred. For images in other formats, please consult with the editors prior to submission. Maximum image size: 1/2 page (approx. 6" wide by 4" tall). Images that do not conform to these guidelines will be rejected.

Copyright

Manuscripts are considered on the understanding that they are not being considered concurrently by another journal. On acceptance you will be asked to assign copyright in your article to the journal. Consent for reproduction of your article in collections of your work appearing subsequent to the publication will be given without charge, contingent on full citation of your article herein.

Electronic Offprints

Authors will receive stand-alone PDFs of their articles, reviews, or letters, which they may freely disseminate in accordance with the provisions of the copyright agreement. Authors will also receive a complete PDF of the Journal issue in which their contributions appear, which in accordance withe copyright agreement is not for dissemination without the explicit permission of Presencing EPIS. Responsibility for Views: Presencing EPIS is published under the auspices of the Existential Psychoanalytic Institute & Society (EPIS). Neither EPIS nor its editorial boards hold themselves responsible for the views expressed by contributors.

Address for Correspondence via email

nazarita66@gmail.com
kbradref@gmail.com

Editorial Office

Presencing EPIS
The Existential Psychoanalytic Institute & Society
2026 S. 9th W., #4
Missoula, Montana 59801 USA
www.episworldwide.com

About EPIS Press

We established EPIS Press in the objective of publishing new work in the following areas of inquiry:

1) existential psychoanalysis & phenomenology;

2) traditional & contemporary psychoanalysis theoretical and clinical;

3) critical philosophy as it pertains to psychoanalysis, culture, phenomenology, and philosophy of mind;

4) new literature in phenomenology and psychoanalysis;

5) any related work as it bears on these issues, including neuropsychology and psychoanalysis.

For more information go to
EPIS Press
2026 S. 9th W., #4
Missoula, MT 59801
epispublishing1@gmail.com
www.episworldwide.com

EPIS RADIO

Radio for the thinking person.

EPIS Radio—Radio for the Thinking Person—has become wildly successful, entertaining discussions in psychoanalysis, phenomenology, Critical Theory, and cultural studies. If you know of a person you think we should interview, please have them contact us. Interviews are informative, valuable, and fun.

episworldwide.com
kbradref@gmail.com

EPIS Radio Programs
The Existential Psychoanalytic Institute & Society

Made in the USA
Monee, IL
04 November 2026

67391567R10105